A DIPLOMATIC
ADVENTURE

"She was in an agony of alarm."

A DIPLOMATIC ADVENTURE

BY

S. WEIR MITCHELL, M.D., LL.D.

NEW YORK
THE CENTURY CO.
1906

THE DE VINNE PRESS

A DIPLOMATIC
ADVENTURE

A DIPLOMATIC ADVENTURE

I

NO man has ever been able to write the history of the greater years of a nation so as to include the minor incidents of interest. They pass unnoted, although in some cases they may have had values influential in determining the course of events. It chanced that I myself was an actor in one of these lesser incidents, when second secretary to our legation in France, during the summer of 1862. I may possibly overestimate the ultimate importance of my adventure, for Mr. Adams, our minister at the court of St. James, seems to have failed to record it, or, at least, there is no allusion to it in his biography. In the perplexing tangle of the diplomacy of the darker days of our civil war, many strange stories must have passed unrecorded, but surely none of those remembered and written were more singular than the occurrences which disturbed the quiet of my uneventful official life in the autumn of 1862.

At this time I had been in the legation two years, and was comfortably lodged in pleasant apartments in the Rue Rivoli.

Somewhere about the beginning of July I had occasion to engage a new servant, and of this it becomes needful to speak because the man I took chanced to play a part in the little drama which at last involved many more important people.

I had dismissed a stout Alsatian because of my certainty that, like his predecessor, he was a spy in the employ of the imperial police. There was little for him to learn; but to feel that I was watched, and, once, that my desk had been searched, was disagreeable. This time I meant to be on safer ground, and was inquiring for a suitable servant when a lean, alert little man presented himself with a good record as a valet in England and France. He was very neat and had a humorous look which caught my fancy. His name was Alphonse Duret. We agreed easily as to wages and that he was to act as valet, take care of my salon, and serve as footman at need. Yes, he could come at once. Upon this I said:

"A word more and I engage you." And then, sure that his reply would be a confident negative, "Are you not a spy in the service of the police?" To my amused surprise he said:

"Yes, but will monsieur permit me to explain?"

"Certainly."

"I was intended by my family to be a priest, but circumstances caused me to make a change. It was not gay."

"Well, hardly."

"I was for a time a valet, but circumstances occurred—monsieur may observe that I am frank. Later I was on the police force, but after two years I fell ill and lost my place. When I was well again, I was taken on as an observer. Monsieur permits me to describe it as an observer?"

"A spy?" I said.

"I cannot contradict monsieur. I speak English—I learned it when I was valet for Mr. Parker in London. That is why I am sent here. The pay is of a minuteness. Circumstances make some addition desirable."

I perceived that circumstances appeared to play a large part in this queer autobiography, and saved the necessity of undesirable fullness of statement.

I said: "You appear to be frank, but are you to belong to me or to the police? In your studies for the priesthood you may have heard that a man cannot serve two masters."

His face became of a sudden what I venture to call luminous with the pleasure an intelligent man has in finding an answer to a difficult question.

He replied modestly: "A man has many masters. One of mine has used me badly. I became ill from exposure in the service, but they refused to take me back. If monsieur will trust me, there shall be but one real master."

The man interested me. I said: "If I engage you, you will, I suppose, desire to remain what you call an observer."

"Yes. Monsieur may be sure that either I or another will observe. Since the unfortunate war in America, monsieur and all others of his legation are watched."

"And generally every one else," I said. "Perhaps you, too, are observed."

"Possibly. Monsieur may perceive that it is better I continue in the pay of the police. It is hardly more than *a pourboire,* but it is desirable. I have an old mother at Neuilly."

I had my doubts in regard to the existence of the mother—but it was true, as I learned later.

"It seems to me," I said, "that you will have to report your observations."

"Yes; I cannot avoid that. Monsieur may feel assured that I shall communicate very important information to my lesser master,"—he grinned,—"in fact, whatever monsieur pleases. If I follow and report at times to the police where monsieur visits, I may be trusted to be at need entirely untrustworthy and prudent. I do not smoke. Monsieur's cigars are safe. If monsieur has absinthe about, I might—monsieur permits me to be suggestive."

The man's gaiety, his intelligence, and his audacious frankness took my fancy. I said: "There is nothing in my life, my man, which is not free for all to know. I shall soon learn whether or not I may trust you. If you are faithful you shall be rewarded. That is all." As I spoke his pleasant face became grave.

"Monsieur shall not be disappointed." Nor was he. Alphonse proved to be a devoted servant, a man with those respectful familiarities which are rare except in French and Italian domestics. When once I asked him how far his superiors had profited by his account of me, he put on a queer, wry face and said circumstances had obliged him to become inventive. He had been highly commended. It seemed as well to inquire no further.

II

ON the 6th of October I found on my table a letter of introduction and the card of Captain Arthur Merton, U.S.A. (2d Infantry), 12 Rue du Roi de Rome.

The note was simple but positive. My uncle, Harry Wellwood, a cynical, pessimistic old bachelor and a rank Copperhead, wrote me to make the captain welcome, which meant much to those who knew my uncle. On that day the evening mail was large. Alphonse laid the letters on my table, and as he lingered I said, "Well, what is it?"

"Monsieur may not observe that three letters from America have been opened in the post-office."

I said, "Yes." In fact, it was common and of course annoying. One of these letters was from my uncle. He wrote:

A Diplomatic Adventure

I gave Arthur Merton an open letter to you, but I add this to state that he is one of the few decent gentlemen in the army of the North.

He inherited his father's share in the mine of which I am part owner, and has therefore no need to serve an evil cause. He was born in New Orleans of Northern parents, spent two years in the School of Mines in Paris, and until this wretched war broke out has lived for some years among mining camps and in the ruffian life of the far West. It is a fair chance which side turns up, the ways of the salon, the accuracy of the man of science, or the savagery of the Rockies. You will like him.

He has been twice wounded, and then had the good sense to acquire the mild typhoid fever which gave him an excuse to ask for leave of absence. He has no diplomatic or political errand, and goes abroad merely to recruit his health. Things here are not yet quite as bad as I could desire to see them. Antietam was unfortunate, but in the end the European States will recognize the South and end the war. I shall then reside in Richmond.

Yours truly,

Harry Wellwood.

I hoped that the imperial government profited by my uncle's letter. It was or may have been of use, as things turned out, in freeing Captain Merton from police observation, which at this time rarely failed to keep under notice every American.

I was kept busy at the legation two thirds of the following day. At five I set out in a coupé having Alphonse on the seat with the coachman. He left cards for me at a half-dozen houses, and then I told him to order the driver to leave me at Rue du Roi de Rome, No. 12.—Captain Merton's address.

As I sat in the carriage and looked out at the exterior gaiety of the open-air life of

Paris, my mind naturally turned in contrast to the war at home and the terrible death harvest of Antietam, news of which had lately reached Europe. The sense of isolation in a land of hostile opinion often oppressed me, and rarely was as despotic as on this afternoon. I turned for relief to speculative thought of the numberless dramas of the lives of the busy multitude among which I drove. I wondered how many lived simple and uneventful days, like mine, in the pursuit of mere official or domestic duties. Not the utmost imaginative ingenuity of the novelist could have anticipated, as I rode along amidst the hurries and the leisures of a Parisian afternoon, that my next hour or two was about to bring into the monotony of office life an adventure as strange as any which I could have conceived as possible for any human unit of these numberless men and women.

Captain Merton lived so far away from the quarter in which I had been leaving cards that it was close to dusk when I got out of the carriage at the hotel I sought.

I meant to return on foot, but hearing thunder, and rain beginning to fall heavily, I told Alphonse to keep the carriage. The captain was not at home. I had taken his card from my pocket to assure me in regard to the address, and as I hurried to reënter my coupé I put it in my card-case for future reference.

III

AS I sat down in the coupé, and Alphonse
was about to close the door, I saw behind
him a lady standing in the heavy downfall of
rain. I said in my best French: "Get in,
madame. I will get out and leave you the carriage." For a moment she hesitated, and then
got in and stood a moment, saying, "Thank
you, but I insist that monsieur does not get
out in the rain." It was just then a torrent.
"Let me leave monsieur where he would desire
to go." I said I intended to go to the Rue de
la Paix, but I added, "If madame has no objection, may I not first drop her wherever she
wishes to go?"

"Oh, no, no! It is far—too far." She was,
as it seemed to me, somewhat agitated. For
a moment I supposed this to be due to the
annoyance a ride with a strange man might

have suggested as compromising, or at least as the Parisian regards such incidents. Alphonse waited calmly, the door still open.

Again I offered to leave her the carriage, and again she refused. I said, "Might I then ask where madame desires to go?"

She hesitated a moment, and then asked irrelevantly, "Monsieur is not French?"

"Oh, no. I am an American."

"And I, too." She showed at once a certain relief, and I felt with pleasure that had I been other than her countryman she would not have trusted me as she did. She added: "On no account could I permit you to get out in this storm. If I ask you to set me down in the Bois—I mean, if not inconvenient—"

"Of course," I replied. "Get up, Alphonse." It was, I thought, a rather vague direction, but there was already something odd in this small adventure. No doubt she would presently be more specific. "The Bois, Alphonse," I repeated. A glance at my countrywoman left with me the impression of a lady, very handsome, about twenty-five, and presumably married. Why she was so very evidently perturbed I could not see. As we drove on I asked her for a more definite direction. She hesitated for a moment and then said Avenue du Bois de Boulogne.

"That will answer," I returned. "But that is only a road, and it is raining hard. You have no umbrella. Surely you do not mean me to drop you on an open road in this storm." I was becoming curious.

"It will do—it will do," she said.

I thought it strange, but I called out the order to Alphonse and bade him promise a good *pourboire*.

As we drove away, all of the many people in the streets were hurrying to take refuge from the sudden and unexpected downfall of heavy rain. Women picked their way with the skill of the Parisienne, men ran for shelter, and the carriages coming in haste from the afternoon drives thronged the great avenue. The scene was not without amusement for people not subject to its inconvenience and to the damage of gay gowns. I made some laughing comment. She made no reply. Presently, however, she took out her purse and said, "Monsieur will at least permit me to—"

"Pardon me," I returned gaily: "I am just now the host, and as it may never again chance that I have the pleasure of madame for a guest, I must insist on my privileges."

For the first time she laughed, as if more at ease, and said, looking up from her purse and flushing a little: "Unluckily, I cannot insist, as I find that I am, for the time, too poor to be proud. I can only pay in thanks. I am glad it is a fellow-countryman to whom I am indebted."

We seemed to be getting on to more agreeable social terms, and I expressed my regret that the torrent outside was beginning to leak in at the window and through the top of the carriage. For a moment she made no remark, and then said with needless emphasis:

"Yes, yes. It is dreadful. I hope—I mean, I trust—that it will never occur again."

It was odd and hardly courteous. I said only, "Yes, it must be disagreeable."

"Oh, I mean—I can't explain—I mean this —special ride, and I—I am so wet."

Of course I accepted this rather inadequate explanation of language which somehow did not seem to me to fit a woman evidently of the best social class. As if she too felt the need to substitute a material inconvenience for a less comprehensible and too abrupt statement, she added: "I am really drenched," and then, as though with a return of some more urgent feeling, "but there are worse things."

I said, "That may very well be." I began to realize as singular the whole of this interview—the broken phrases which I could not interpret, the look of worry, the embarrassment of long silences.

After a time, at her request, we turned into

one of the smaller avenues. Meanwhile I
made brief efforts at impersonal talk—the
rain, the vivid lightning,—wondering if it
were the latter which made her so nervous.
She murmured short replies, and at last I gave
up my efforts at talk, and we drove on in
silence, the darkness meanwhile coming the
sooner for the storm.

By and by she said, "I owe you an apology
for my preoccupation. I am—I have reason
to be—troubled. You must pardon my silence."

Much surprised, I acquiesced with some
trifling remark, and we went on, neither of us
saying a word, while the rain beat on the leaky
cover of the carriage, and now and then I
heard a loud "Sacré!" from the coachman as
the lightning flashed.

It was now quite dark. We were far across
the Bois and in a narrow road. To set her
more at ease, I was about to tell her my name
and official position, when of a sudden she
cried:

"Oh, monsieur, we are followed! I am sure we are followed. What shall I do?"

Here was a not very agreeable adventure.

I said, "No, I think not."

However, I did hear a carriage behind us; and as she persisted, I looked back and saw through the night the lamps of what I took to be a cabriolet.

As at times we moved more slowly, so it seemed did the cabriolet; and when our driver, who had no lights, saw better at some open place and went faster, so did the vehicle behind us. I felt sure that she was right, and to reassure her said: "We have two horses. He has one. We ought to beat him." I called to Alphonse to tell the driver to drive as fast as he could and he should have a napoleon. He no doubt comprehended the situation, and began to lash his horses furiously. Meantime the woman kept ejaculating, *"Mon Dieu!"* and then, in English, "Oh, I am so afraid! What shall we do?" I said, "I will take care of you." How, I did not know.

It was an awkward business—probably a jealous husband; but there was no time to ask for explanations, nor was I so inclined. It seemed to me that we were leaving our pursuers, when again I heard the vehicle behind us, and, looking back, saw that it was rapidly approaching, and then, from the movement of the lanterns, that the driver in trying to overtake us must have lost control of his horse, as the lights were now on this side of the road, now on that. My driver drew in to the left, close to the wood, thinking, I presume, that they would pass us.

A moment later there was a crash. One of our horses went down, and the cabriolet—the lighter vehicle—upset, falling over to the right. As we came to a standstill I threw open the left-hand door saying: "Get out, madame! Quick! Into the wood!" She was out in an instant and, favored by the gloom, was at once lost to sight among the thick shrubbery. I shut the door and got out on the other side.

It was very dark and raining hard as I saw Alphonse slip away into the wood shadows. Next I made out the driver of the cabriolet, who had been thrown from his seat and was running up to join us.

In a moment I saw more clearly. The two coachmen were swearing, the horses down, the two vehicles, as it proved later, not much injured. A man was standing on the farther side of the roadway. I went around the fallen cab and said: "An unlucky accident, monsieur. I hope you are not hurt." He was holding a handkerchief to his head.

"No, I am not much hurt."

"I am well pleased," said I, " that it is no worse." I expected that the presumably jealous husband would at once make himself unpleasant. To my surprise, he stood a moment without speaking, and, as I fancied, a little dazed by his fall. Then he said:

"There is a woman in that carriage."

I was anxious to gain time for the fugitive, and replied: "Monsieur must be under some singular misapprehension. There is no one in my carriage."

"I shall see for myself," he said sharply.

"By all means. I am quite at a loss to understand you." I was sure that he would not be able to see her.

He staggered as he moved past me, and was evidently more hurt than he was willing to admit. I went quickly to my coachman, who was busy with a broken trace. Here was the trouble—the risk. I bent over him and whispered, putting a napoleon in his hand, "There was no woman in the carriage."

"Two," said the rascal.

"Well, two if you will lie enough."

"Good! This *sacré* animal! Be quiet!"

I busied myself helping the man, and a moment later the gentleman went by me and, as I expected, asked the driver. "There was a woman in your carriage?"

"No, monsieur; the gentleman was alone,

and you have smashed my carriage. *Sacré bleu!* Who is to pay?"

"That is of no moment. Here is my card."

The man took it, but said doubtfully, "That 's all well to-day, but to-morrow—"

"Stuff! Your carriage is not damaged. Here, my man, a half-napoleon will more than pay."

The driver, well pleased with this accumulation of unlooked-for good fortune, expressed himself contented. The gentleman stood, mopping the blood from his forehead, while the two drivers set up the cabriolet and continued to repair the broken harness. Glad of the delay, I too, stood still in the rain saying nothing. My companion of the hour was as silent.

At last the coachmen declared themselves ready to leave. Upon this, the gentleman said to me: "You have denied, monsieur, that there was a woman with you. It is my belief that she has escaped into the wood."

"I denied nothing," said I. "I invited you to look for yourself. The wood is equally at your disposal. I regret—or, rather I do not regret—to be unable to assist you."

Then, to my amazement, he said: "You, too, are in this affair, I presume. You will find it serious."

"What affair? Monsieur is enigmatical and anything but courteous."

"You are insulting, and my friends will ask you to-morrow to explain your conduct. I think you will further regret your connection with this matter."

"With what matter?" I broke in. "This passes endurance."

"I fancy you need no explanation. I presume that at least you will not hesitate to inform me of your name."

As he spoke his coachman called out to him to hold his horse for a moment, and before I could answer, he turned aside toward the man. I followed him, took out my card-case, and said as I gave him a card, "This will sufficiently inform you who and what I am."

As I spoke he in turn gave me his card, saying: "I am the Count le Moyne. I shall have the honor to ask through my friends for an explanation."

He was evidently somewhat cooler. As he spoke I knew his name as that of a recently appointed under-secretary of the Foreign Office. I had never before seen him. As we parted I said:

"I shall be at home from eleven until noon to-morrow."

We lifted our hats, and the two carriages having been put in condition, I drove away, with enough to think about and with some wonder as to what had become of Alphonse.

IV

AFTER a slow drive with a lame horse I reached my club, where I attended to a small matter, and then, as the rain was over, walked to my rooms. A bath and a change of garments left me free to consider the adventure and its too probable results. What was meant by the affair? It was really a somewhat bewildering business.

I looked at the count's card. His name was, as I have said, somewhat unfamiliar, although it was part of duty at our legation to learn all I could in the upper social life of Paris where, at this time, we had few friends and many foes. If, still unsatisfied, he chose to look up my driver, I felt that the man would readily tell all he knew. The count had said I was in the affair. A confederate? What affair? I

could not—indeed, I did not mean to—explain
how I came to be with the woman, nor to admit that there was a woman concerned. There
had been, however, enough to make me sure
that in that case I might have to face a duel,
and that the next day I should hear from this
angry gentleman. But who was my handsome and terrified companion, and what was
the affair?

To refuse to meet him would be social ruin
and would seriously affect my usefulness, as I
was the only attaché who spoke French with
entire ease, and it was, as I said, a part of my
duty to learn at the clubs and in society the
trend of opinion in regard to the war with
the rebel States. I could do nothing but wait.
I was the victim of circumstances and of an
embarrassing situation not of my making, and
in regard to which I could offer no explanation. There was nothing left for me except
to see what the morning would bring.

I dined that evening with my chief, but of

course said nothing of my adventure. On my return home I found Alphonse.

"Well," I said, "what the deuce became of you?"

"I dived into the edge of the wood, and after hearing what passed I considered that you might desire to know who the lady was."

"Yes, I did—I do."

"I overtook her very easily, and as she seemed quite lost, I said I was your servant. When I had set her on the avenue she wanted to find, she said I might go, and gave me a napoleon, and I was to thank you."

"Did you follow her?"

"No; she seemed to want to go on alone. I hope monsieur approves."

"I do."

There was a curious delicacy about this which was explained when he added: "She is quite sure to let monsieur hear of her again. I ventured to mention your name."

The point of view was Parisian enough, but

I contented myself with a further word of satisfaction, although I had my doubts as to whether his theory would fit the case of my handsome countrywoman.

As I rose, about to go to bed, I said to Alphonse: "You will find in my card-case the card and address of Captain Merton. I shall want you to take a note to him in the morning."

He came back with the case in his hand and said: "I saw you take out a card, sir, when we were at 12 Rue du Roi de Rome. You looked at it and put it back in the case. It is not there now, nor in any of your pockets, but I remember the address. Perhaps—" and he paused.

"Perhaps what?"

"You gave the very angry gentleman a card."

"Nonsense!" I returned. "Look again." I could see, by the faint smile and the slight uplift of the brow, that my valet appreciated the situation. He was gone for at least ten minutes. Meanwhile I sat still, more and more sure that I had made one of those blunders which might bear unpleasant interpretations. At length, impatient, I joined Alphonse in his search. It was vain. He stood at last facing me with a pair of pantaloons on one arm, a coat on the other, all the pockets turned inside out.

"Monsieur—circumstances—I mean it is to be feared—I have looked everywhere."

"It is incredible," said I.

"But the night, monsieur, and the storm, and the count, who was not polite."

He was sorry for me and perfectly understood what had happened. Yes, undoubtedly I had given the count Captain Merton's card. I said as much while Alphonse stood still with a look in which his constant sense of the comic contended for expression with his desire to sympathize in what he was shrewd enough to know was, for me, that form of the socially tragic which has for its catastrophe ridicule.

I went back to my salon and sat down to reflect on the consequences of my mishap. Of
course, it was easy to set the matter right, but
what a muddle! I must make haste in the
morning to correct my blunder.

Desirous to be on time, about ten the next
morning I called on the count. He had gone
out. At the Foreign Office I again failed to
find him. I was told that he had gone to his
club for breakfast, but would be back very
shortly. I waited a half-hour and then tried
the club. He had left. Remembering that I
had said I should be at home from eleven to
twelve, I looked at my watch and saw, to my
annoyance, that it was close to noon. I had
hoped to anticipate the call of the count's
seconds on Merton. I felt sure, however, that
the captain would simply deny any share in
my adventure, and that a word or a note from
me to the count would set things straight. Although I regretted the delay my vain pursuit
of the count had caused, a little reflection put
me at ease, and calling a cab, I drove to Cap-

tain Merton's. I was so fortunate as to find him at home. As I entered he threw on the table a number of letters and made me welcome with a certain cordiality which in its manner had both refinement and the open-air frankness of a dweller in camps.

I liked him from the first, and being myself a small man, envied the six feet one of well-knit frame, and was struck with a way he had of quick backward head movement when the large blue eyes considered you with smiling attention. My first impression was that nothing as embarrassing as the absurd situation in which my blunder might have placed him could as yet have fallen upon this tranquil gentleman. There was therefore no occasion for haste.

We talked pleasantly of home, the war, my uncle, and Paris, and I was about to mention my mistake in regard to his card when he said rather abruptly:

"I should like you to advise me as to a rather odd affair—if not too late for advice.

"About eleven to-day, the Baron la Garde and a Colonel St. Pierre called upon me on the part of a certain Count le Moyne. The baron explained that, as a lady was involved, it would be better if it were supposed that we had quarreled at cards. As you may imagine, I rather surprised, and asked what he meant. He replied, and not very pleasantly, that I must know, as I had given my card to the count and said I should be at home from eleven to twelve. I said: 'Pardon me, gentlemen, but there is some mistake. I do not know Count le Moyne, and I never saw him. As to my card—I have given no one my card.' I was, of course, very civil and quiet in my denial, and the more so because the baron's manner was far from agreeable.

"Then the baron, to my amazement, handed me my own card, saying, 'Do we understand you to say that last night, in the Bois de Boulogne, you did not give Count le Moyne your card?'

"Now I am at times, Mr. Greville, short of

temper, and the supply was giving out. I checked myself, however, and said as calmly as possible: 'Really, gentlemen, this is a rather absurd. I was at home last night. I never saw or heard of your count, and you will be so good as to accept for him my absolute denial.'

"Upon this the baron said, 'It appears to us that you contradict flatly the statement of our principal, a man of the highest character, and that we are therefore forced to suppose that you are endeavoring to escape the consequence of having last night insulted the count.'

"Before I could reply, the other man—the colonel—remarked in a casual way that there was only one word to characterize my conduct. Here I broke in—but, for a wonder, kept myself in hand.

"I said: 'This has gone far enough. Count le Moyne has rather imprudent friends. Some one has played me and your principal a trick. At all events, I am not the man.'

" 'Monsieur,' said the colonel, 'so you still deny—'

" 'Wait a little,' said I. 'I allow no man to doubt my word. But let us be clear as to this. Am I to understand that the language now used to me represents the instructions of the count?'

"By George! the colonel said, 'Yes.' They really believed me to be lying. I had gotten past any desire to explain or contradict, and so I replied that it was all damn nonsense, but that I had supposed French gentlemen were on these occasions courteous.

. "You should have seen the baron. He is as tall as I am, and must weigh two hundred and fifty pounds. He got red and said that if it were not for his principal's prior claim on me, he should himself at once call me to account. I replied sweetly that need not interfere, for that, after I had killed the count, I should be most glad to accommodate his friend. He did seem a bit amazed."

V

I WAS about to comment on this queer story when Merton said:

"Pardon me, I must first tell you all; then you will kindly say what you think of this amazing performance.

"The little colonel, who had the leanness and redness of a boiled shrimp, now took up the talk, and this other idiot said: 'My friend the baron will, no doubt, postpone the pleasure of meeting monsieur; and now, as monsieur is no longer indisposed to satisfy our principal, and, as we understand it, declines to explain or apologize,—in fact, admits, by his inclination to meet our friend, what he seemed to deny,—may we have the honor to know when monsieur' seconds will wait on us? Here is my card.'

"The little man was posing beautifully. I

laid his card on the table and said, 'Be so good, gentlemen, as to understand that I have not retracted my statement, but that if the count insists, as you do, that I lie,—that, at least, is decent cause for a quarrel,—he can have it.'

"The little man replied that the count could not do otherwise.

" 'Very good,' said I.—No, don't interrupt this charming story, Mr. Greville; let me go on. There is more of it and better.

"My colonel then said, 'We shall expect to hear from you—and, by the way, I understand from monsieur's card that he is an American.'

"I said, 'Yes; captain Second Infantry.'

" 'Ah, a soldier—really! In the army of the Confederation, I presume. We shall be enchanted to meet monsieur's friends.'

" 'What!' I said; 'does monsieur the colonel wish to insult me? I am of the North.'

" 'A thousand pardons!'

" 'No matter. You will hear from me

shortly, or as soon as I am able to find gentlemen who will be my seconds.' This seemed to
suit them until I remarked that, to save time,
being the challenged party, I might as well
say that my friends would insist on the rifle at
thirty paces.

" 'But monsieur, that is unusual, barbarous!' said the little man.

" 'Indeed!' said I 'Then suppose we say
revolvers at twelve paces or less. I have no
prejudices.' It seems that the baron had, for
he said my new proposition was also unheard
of, uncivilized.

"Upon this I stood up and said: 'Gentlemen, you have insisted on manufacturing for
me a quarrel with a man I never saw, and have
suggested—indeed, said—that I, a soldier, am
afraid and have lied to you. I accepted the
situation thus forced on me, and in place of
the wretched little knitting-needles with which
you fight child duels in France, I propose to
take it seriously.'

"I saw the little man—the colonel—was beginning to fidget. As I stopped he said, 'Pardon me; I have not the honor fully to comprehend.'

" 'Indeed?' said I. 'So far I have hesitated to ascribe to gentlemen, to a soldier, any motive for your difficulty in accepting weapons which involve peril, and I thought that I had at last done so. I do not see how I can make myself more clear.'

" 'Sir,' said my little man, 'do I understand—'

"I was at the end of the sweetest temper west of the Mississippi. I broke into English and said: 'You may understand what you damn please.'

"You see, Mr. Greville, it was getting to be fatiguing—these two improbable Frenchmen. I suppose the small man took my English as some recondite insult, for he drew himself up, clicked his heels together, and said, 'I shall have the honor to send to monsieur those who will ask him, for me,—for me, personally,—to translate his words, and, I trust, to withdraw the offensive statement which, no doubt, they are meant to convey.'

"I replied that I had no more to say, except that I should instruct my friends to abide by the weapons I had mentioned. On this he lost his temper and exclaimed that it was murder. I said that was my desire; that they were hard to please; and that bowie-knives exhausted the list of weapons I should accept.

"The colonel said further that, as I seemed to be ignorant of the customs of civilized countries, it appeared proper to let me know that the seconds were left to settle these preliminaries, and he supposed that I was making a jest of a grave situation.

"When I replied that he was as lacking in courtesy as the baron, the little man became polite and regretted that the prior claim of of his two friends would, he feared, deprive him of the pleasure of exacting that satisfaction which he still hoped circumstances would eventually afford him. He was queerly percise and too absurd for belief.

"I replied lightly that I should be sorry if any accident were to deprive him of the happiness of meeting me, but that I had the pleasant hope of being at his service after I had shot the count and the baron. I began to enjoy this unique situation.

"The colonel said I was most amiable—but really, my dear Mr. Greville, it is past my power to do justice to this scene. They were like the Count Considines and the Irish gentlemen in Lever's novels."

"And was that all?" I asked.

"No, not quite. After the colonel ceased to criticize my views of the duel, he again informed me that his own friends would call upon me to withdraw my injurious language. Then these two peacemakers departed. Now what do you think of my comedy?"

I had listened in amazement to this arrangement—three duels as the sequel of my adventure! As Merton ended, he burst into a roar of laughter.

"Now," he said, "what will they do?—rifle, revolver, or bowie? By George, I am like d'Artagnan—my second day in Paris and three duels on my hands! Is n't it jolly?"

That was by no means my opinion. "Mr. Merton," I said, "I came here about this very matter."

"Indeed! How can that be? Pray go on—and did any man ever hear of such a mix-up? Where do you come in?"

"I will tell you. Last night in the dark, by mishap, I gave this infernal count your card instead of my own."

"The deuce you did! Great Scott, what fun!"

"Yes, I did." I went on to relate my encounter with the lady, and the manner in which Count le Moyne had behaved.

"What an adventure! I am so sorry I was not in your place. What a fine mystery! But

what will you do? Was she his wife? I have
had many adventures, but nothing to compare
with this. I envy you. And you were sure
she was not his wife?"

"No, she was not his wife; and as to what I
shall do, it is simple. I shall go to the count
and explain the card and my mistake. I
meant to anticipate the visit to you of Count
le Moyne's seconds. I am sorry to have been
late."

"Sorry! Not I. It is immense!"

"The count will call me out. There will be
the usual farce of a sword duel. I am in fair
practice. This will relieve you so far as con-
cerns the count, and nobody else will fight you
with the weapons you offer."

"Won't they, indeed? I have been insulted.
Do you suppose I can sit quiet under it? No,
Mr. Greville. You, I hope, may make yourself unpleasant to this count, but I shall settle
with him and the others, too. Did I happen
to mention that I told them I did not fight
with knitting-needles?"

"You did."

"They seemed annoyed."

"Probably," said I. Although the whole affair appeared to me comical, it had, too, its possible tragedy.

"Well," I continued, "I shall find the count, and set right the matter of the cards. After that we may better see our way. These matters are never hurried over here. Dine with me to-night at my rooms at seven-thirty; and meanwhile, as for the baron—"

"Oh, the baron—you should see him. I came near to calling him Porthos to his face. I wish I had."

"And the small man, the colonel—"

"Oh, yes—shade of Dumas! He may pass for Aramis."

I laughed. "By the way," I added, "he is one of the best blades in France."

"Is he? However he comes in third. But can he shoot? If I accept the sword,—and it may come to that,—I am pretty sure to be left

with something to remember. If we use rifles,
I assure you they will remember me still longer
or not at all." There was savage menace in
his blue eyes as he spoke. "But is it not
ridiculous?"

I said it was.

"And now about this count who is interested in the anonymous lady. I suppose he
may pass for Athos. That makes it complete.
Have some rye. Smuggled it. Said it was
medicine. The customs fellow tried it neat,
and said I had poisoned him."

I declined the wine of my country, and answered him that Athos, as I had learned, was,
a man of high character who had lately joined
the Foreign Office, a keen imperialist, happily
married and rich.

"Then certainly it cannot be the wife."

"No, I think I said so; I am thankful to be
able to say that it is not. But what part the
woman has in this muddle is past my compre-
hension."

"Stop a little," said my d'Artagnan. "You are having a good deal of trouble to keep this short-legged Emperor from getting John Bull and the rest to bully us into peace."

"Yes, there has been trouble brewing all summer." I could not imagine what the man was after.

"Well, the woman seemed pleased when she learned that you were an American. You said so, and also that the count charged you with being in that affair. He slipped up a bit there. He seemed to believe you to be engaged in something of which he did not want to talk freely."

"Yes, that is true."

The blue eyes held mine for a moment, and then he inquired, "Was she—" and he paused.

"My dear captain, she is an American and a lady."

"I ask her pardon. A lady? You are sure she is a lady?"

"Yes."

"Then it is a matter of—let me think—not jealousy? Hardly. We may leave that out."

"Certainly."

"Don't you catch on, Mr. Greville?"

"No, I must say I do not."

"Well, consider it coolly. Exclude love, jealousy, any gross fraud, and what is left? What can be left?"

"I do not know."

"How about politics," he smiled. "How does that strike you?"

The moment he let fall this key-word, "Politics," I began to suspect that he was right. The woman had exhibited relief when I had said I was an American. We lived in a maze of spies of nearly every class of life, rarely using the post-office, trusting no one. With our own secret agents I had little to do. The first secretary or the minister saw them, and we were not badly served either in England or

France; but all this did not do more than enable me to see my d'Artagnan's notion as possibly a reasonable guess.

After a moment's thought I said: "You may be right; but even if you are, the matter remains a problem which we are very unlikely ever to solve. But how can a handsome young American woman be so deeply concerned in some political affair as to account for this amazing conduct of a secretary not yet a week old in the work of the imperial Foreign Office."

Merton smiled. "We exhaust personal motives—what else is left? Politics! She may know something which it seems to be desirable she should not know. We must find her."

The more I considered his theory, the more I inclined to doubt it. At all events as things stood it was none of our business—and after a moment's reflection I said:

"We have quite enough on our hands without the woman. I shall see the count to-day, and then we may be in a better position to know what further should be done."

"Done?" laughed the captain. "I shall give all three fools what is called satisfaction. I don't take much stock in them. I hate Aramis. It's the woman interests me the most."

"The woman? I assure you, I am out of that."

"Oh, no, no! We must find her. She is in trouble."

I laughed. "Can we find her?"

"We must. I like her looks."

"But you never saw her."

"No. But the most beautiful woman is always the one I never saw."

He was delightful, my d'Artagnan, with his amused acceptance of three duels, and now his interest in an unknown woman. But I held fast to my opinion, and after some further talk I went away to make my belated explanation to Count le Moyne.

VI

AFTER dinner that evening Merton and I settled ourselves in my little salon with coffee, cognac, and cigars. Merton said:

"Are we safe here?"

"Yes. There are two doors, and the outer one I have locked. My last valet was a spy. The information he got for their Foreign Office must have been valuable. My present man—the fellow who waited on us just now— is also a spy," and upon this I told the captain of my arrangement with Alphonse.

He was much amused. "Can you really trust him?" he said.

"Yes, he has an old mother whom I have seen and have helped. I believe that it is his desire and interest to serve me and at the same time to keep his place as a paid spy."

[52]

"What a droll arrangement! And are you really sure of him?"

"Yes, as far as one can be sure of any one in this tangle of spies."

"But does he not—must he not—seem to earn his outside pay?"

"Yes, seem. I will call him in. He will talk if I assure him that he is safe."

"Delightful—most delightful! By all means!"

I rang for Alphonse.

"Alphonse," I said, " this gentleman is my friend. He cannot quite believe that you can be true to me and yet satisfy your superiors in the police."

"Oh, monsieur!" exclaimed Alphonse. He was evidently hurt.

"To relieve him, tell monsieur of our little arrangement."

"The letters, monsieur?"

"Yes."

"Well, my master is kind enough to leave

open certain letters. They have been found to be of interest. My pay has been raised. Circumstances make it desirable."

"What is her name?" said Merton, laughing.

"Louise."

"What letters, Greville, do you turn over for the recreation and service of the Foreign Office?"

"My uncle's," said I, "usually."

"Ah, I see. The old gentleman's opinions must be refreshing—authoritative they are, I am sure. When last I saw him he had, as usual, secret intelligence from the army. He always has. I think with joy of the effect of his letters on the young secretaries of the Foreign Office."

I confessed my own pleasure in the game, and was about to let Alphonse go when Merton said:

"May I take a great liberty?"

"Certainly," I laughed—"short of taking Alphonse. What is it?"

"Alphonse," asked Merton, "would you know the lady you followed and guided that night in the Bois?"

"Yes, monsieur."

"Do you want to make two hundred francs?"

"Without doubt."

"Find that woman and I will give you three hundred."

"It will be difficult. Paris is large and women are numerous."

"Yes, but there is the Count le Moyne as a clue."

"Yes, yes." He seemed to be thinking. Then he turned to me.

"If monsieur approves and can do without me for two days?"

"Certainly." I was not very anxious to add the woman to our increasing collection of not easily solved problems, but Merton was so eager that I decided to make this new move in our complicated game.

Alphonse stood still a moment.

"Well?" I said.

"The lady, monsieur,—she is, I think, not French."

"No; she is an American, and that is all we know."

"But that is much. Then I am free to-morrow?"

"Yes," and he left us.

"What a fine specimen!" said the captain; "scamp rather than scoundrel. Well, I suppose I shall hear from the count and Porthos and the little man with the pink kid gloves—Aramis. I hate the little animal, but Porthos—I want you to see Porthos. He has gigantic manners. He is so conscious of his bigness, and makes chests at you like a pouter pigeon. He has a bass voice like a war-drum. Things shake. Oh, I like Porthos. Pardon my nonsense, Greville, but the whole thing is so big, so grotesquely huge. Tell me about Athos, the count. Your cigars were not bought in France; may I have another? Thanks. You were to see him to-day."

"Yes; I called on him, and I assure you," I replied, "that nothing you have told me is more wonderful than my sequel. I did think you had the original *trois mousquetaires* rather too much on your mind, but really, the resemblance is certainly fascinating."

"But what about the count? You have seen him, I suppose."

"Yes, I saw Count le Moyne. He lives in a charming little hôtel near the Parc Monceaux. He had my card in his hand when I entered. He welcomed me quite warmly, and said, 'It is odd, as you are of your legation, that we have never met; but then I am only of late transferred from Vienna. Pray sit down.'

"I was sure that for a fraction of a moment he did not identify me, but as I spoke, my voice, as so often happens, revealed more than

the darkness had made visible. I observed at
once that, although still extremely courteous,
he became more cool and looked puzzled.

"I said: 'Monsieur, last night, in the darkness, I gave you by mistake the card of my
friend Captain Merton in place of my own. I
have called in person solely to apologize for
my blunder.' As I spoke I stood up, adding,
'As this is my only purpose, I shall leave you
to rearrange matters as may seem best to
you.' "

VII

AS I turned to go he said: 'May I ask you to sit down? Now that I know you to be of your legation, and I being, as you are aware, in the Foreign Office, an affair between us would be for both services unadvisable. Having left myself in the hands of my friends, I am now doing, as you will understand, an unusual thing; but whatever may be the result, I feel that, as a gentleman, you will hold me excused. There *was* a woman in your carriage. Of course our police found the cabman and got it out of him. I have no direct personal interest in her—none; nor can I explain myself further. I regret that in the annoyance of my failure to effect my purpose I was guilty of a grave discourtesy.

If you had told me that you would send your seconds to me to-day, I should have felt that you were fully justified. I can very well afford to say that I owe you an apology; and, fortunately, my friends will have learned that I sent them to the wrong man and will return for instructions. If, however, you feel—'

" 'Oh, no,' I said; 'pardon me, I am quite willing to forget an unfortunate incident, and to add that the lady, by the merest accident, took shelter from the rain in my carriage. I never met her before.'

"I saw at once that he had a look of what I took to be relief. He smiled, became quite cordial, and when I added that whatever I might have said or done the night before was really unavoidable, he returned that it was quite true that he had been hasty, and that, as he had said very little to his friends, it would rest between us.

"As I rose to go, I could not help saying

[60]

that the remarkably good looks of the woman made my conduct the more excusable.

" 'Yes,' he said; 'at least she is handsome, but—' and here he paused and then added, 'I hope before long to have the pleasure of presenting you to my wife.'

"I thanked him."

"One moment," said Merton, "before you go on. It is clear that the woman is a lady; that he was wildly eager to catch her, and especially at that time; that, being foiled, he lost his temper; that he believes you, or makes believe to do so; and, finally, that he is sensible enough to know that a duel with an American secretary is undesirable. You let him off easy."

"I did, but I had the same kind of reason to avoid a hostile meeting that he has. Moreover, he is really a charming fellow, and it must have cost him something to apologize."

"But about the woman who set all these pots a-boiling—I beg pardon, simmering—"

"Oh, the woman. I hope I may never see her again."

"You will. That fellow Alphonse will find her."

"I hope not. But what a mess! *cherchez la femme!*"

"That we must do," laughed Merton. "The mosquitoes illustrate the proverb: only the females bite. Good, that, is n't it? But what next? I interrupted you. You are out of it, but where do I come in? What about Porthos and that little red weasel Aramis?"

"And D'Artagnan?" I laughed.

"If you like, Greville. You are complimentary. Was that all?"

"No. The count said, 'I will at once write to Captain Merton and apologize, but I fancy my friends have already done so.' I was about to take leave of the count when in walked the baron, behind the biggest mustache in Paris, a ponderous person. 'Shade of Dumas!' I muttered; 'Porthos! Porthos!'

Behind him was a much-made-up little fellow, the colonel—your Aramis."

"Oh, drop him. He is what the arithmeticians call a negligible quantity. What next?"

"The count said, 'Allow me to present M. Greville of the American Legation—the Baron la Garde, my cousin, and the Colonel St. Pierre.' We bowed, and the count said, 'M. Greville is somewhat concerned in the affair in which you have been so kind as to act for me.'

"The two gentlemen looked a little bewildered, but bowed again and sat down, while the count added: 'You may speak freely. I suppose M. Merton explained that he was not the person.' "

"Oh, by all that 's jolly! what a situation for the stage! A match, please. What next?"

"The baron spoke first. 'I do not understand you, my dear count.'

"The count said: 'Why not? It was very simple. I presume you to have said that you regretted the mistake, and then I suppose you apologized and came away to report to me. I am sorry to have sent you on a fruitless errand. Kindly tell us what passed.'

"The colonel sat up, and, as I thought, was a little embarrassed. He said: 'With your permission, baron, I shall have the honor to relate our conversation. We put the matter, count, as you desired. You had been insulted. What explanation had M. Merton to offer? Then this amazing American said that it was not true that he had insulted you; that he had not given you his card; that he had never seen you; that it was a droll mistake—"that you were unfortunate in your friends." I think I am correct, baron?'

" 'Yes. I so understood it.'

" 'Then you said, as I recall it, baron,

that—that—there was only one word to
apply to a man who could insult another and
try to escape the consequences. Then he
said—well, to cut it short, he would send
his friends to us, and that, as he was the
challenged party, it would save time if he
now declared it must be rifles—or revolvers
—or, yes, what he called bowie. What that
is I know not.' "

"Lovely!" murmured Merton. "Go on."

"I explained to the count's friends that
the bowie was a big knife with which our
Western gentlemen chopped one another.
The count sat still, with a look of repressed
mirth, I choking with the fun of it, Aramis
fidgeting, the baron swelling with rage.
The count asked if that were all.

"Aramis went on: 'When I assured M.
Merton that the methods proposed were
barbarous, he made himself unpleasant, and
I was forced to say that his language was
of such incorrectness—in fact, so monstrous

that as a French soldier I held him personally responsible. The animal assured me
that when he was through with you and the
baron, he would attend to my own case. I
grieve to admit, count, that our friend the
baron, usually so amiable, had previously
lost his temper. That was when our brig-
and proposed revolvers and the knife-bowie,
and said we were difficult.'

" 'I did,' said the baron; 'I, who am all
that there is of amiable. Yes, I lost my
temper.' He stood up as he went on. 'I
said it was uncivilized, that it was no jest,
but a grave matter. *Mon Dieu!* That man,
he told me that we fought with knitting-
needles, that our duels were baby-play—me
—me—he said that to me! What could I reply? I said I should ask him to retract.
That man laughed—*à faire peur*—the room
shook. Then he said to excuse him, it was
—so what he called "damn nonsense." I
think, colonel, I am correct? What means
that, M. Greville—damn nonsense?'

" 'English for very interesting,' said I,
not wishing to aggravate the situation.

" 'Ah, thanks,' said Aramis. 'This American he was pleasant of a sudden, and would
be happy to hear from us all. He did regret that I came third, but that after he
had killed you and the baron he would be
most happy to kill me. *Mon Dieu!* we shall
see. It remains to await his friends. I
shall kill him.'

" 'Pardon me,' said the baron; 'he belongs
to me.'

"Meanwhile the count's face was a study.
What it cost him not to explode into laughter I shall never guess except by my knowl-
edge of the internal convulsions of my own
organs of mirth. But Athos—I like him.
He said at last very quietly: 'Here, gentlemen, are three duels—a fair morning's work.
May I ask you, M. Greville, if you know
Captain Merton? I mean well.' "

"Lord, what a chance! What did you
say?"

"I saw what he meant, and said you were a captain in our army, had been twice wounded, and were here to recruit your health; that you were of first force with the rifle and revolver, but knew nothing of the small sword.

"The baron's shoulders were lifted and he spread out huge hands of disgust. 'But these weapons are impossible. Only a semi-civilized people could desire to employ the weapons of savages.'

" 'Pardon me,' I said; 'I presume that the rifle and revolver are both used in your service; and, also, may I ask you to remember that I, too, am an American?'

" 'That does not alter my opinion. If monsieur—'

" 'Oh, stop, stop!' cried the count. 'M. Greville is my guest. He will allow me to reply. Do you mean to create four duels in a day? My dear cousin will recall his words.'

"'My dear cousin' did not like it, but said stiffly, 'So far as M. Greville is concerned, I withdraw them.'

"I bowed and said: 'Permit me, count. These gentlemen, as it seems to me, have put you and themselves in the position of challengers, which everywhere gives to the challenged party the right to choose his weapon. As M. Merton's friends will abide by his decision, your own seconds must, I fancy, accept what is or would be usual with us. They have no choice except to decline and allow their refusal to be made public, as it will be, or to choose one of the three weapons so generously offered.'

"The baron glared at me, the colonel was silent, and the count said: 'M. Greville is correct. I regret to have been the means of putting you in a false position. M. Greville has come to explain to me that in the darkness of the night, when our vehicles came together and we said some angry words, he gave me by mistake the card of M. le Capitaine Merton. M. Greville and I—you will pardon me—have amicably arranged our little trouble, as I shall tell you more fully.' "

"Oh, joy!" cried Merton; "close of fourth act. Every one on but D'Artagnan and the woman. Athos, Porthos, Aramis! What next? Was there ever anything more dramatically all that could be desired? What next?"

"The count was very pleasant, and thought only a little explanation was required to reconcile his friends and the captain. This by no means satisfied Porthos.

"The baron said he would fight with a cannon if necessary, and he will. Aramis is degenerate. He observed that it would require consideration. Then the count said: 'The captain's ideas are certainly somewhat original, and why not leave it to M. Greville and me and such others as we may choose?'

"I was well pleased. Whether they were or not, I cannot tell. They said, however, a variety of agreeable nothings, and I am to see the count to-morrow. He kept Porthos and Aramis and, I suspect, gave the two fools a lecture."

"Well, well," said Merton. "When I left the regiment I thought I was out of the world of adventure."

"Oh, this is comic opera. I do not suppose that you really want to fight these idiots."

"No; but I will, if they desire to be thus amused. Otherwise there will have to be some word-eating. I was not bluffing."

"Porthos will stick it out. You won't be too stiff-necked, I trust."

"Oh, no. I leave myself in your hands— I mean absolutely; and I want also to say, Greville, that this queer affair ought to make us friends."

"It has," I returned with warmth. "You dine with the minister next week, I believe."

"Yes, Monday."

We talked for a few minutes of the campaigns at home, and then he returned to the subject which just now more immediately interested him. "What about that woman? I have an impression that we are not at the end, but at the beginning, of an adventure. Are you not curious?"

"Yes, I am, and my curiosity has ripened. There may be some politics in the matter, just as you say. If, as is barely possible, it is our international affairs that are involved, it is my duty to follow it up and to know more. But how to follow it up? In what way an unknown American lady can be concerned in them, I am unable to imagine. This, however, is, I think, certain, the count did not want to be involved in an affair of honor about this lady. We were to be supposed to have quarreled over cards. He wanted her to disappear from the scene. But why?"

"Well, it is late," said Merton, looking at the clock. "Good night. I shall stay at home to-morrow until I hear from you and the count."

I may add that Merton at once accepted the count's explanation and called on him. The affair of Baron Porthos and my friend proved more difficult. Both declined to apologize. Somehow, it got out at the clubs, and Paris was gaily amused over para-graphs about the Wild West man who would fight only with the knife-bowie. Merton was furious, and I had hard work to keep him within bounds.

Meanwhile the count and another gentle-man met me, a friend of mine, Lieutenant West, a naval officer, and made vain efforts to bring about peace or a duel with swords; at which Merton only laughed, saying that when he went "a-cat-fishing, he went a-cat-fishing," a piece of national wisdom which I found myself incompetent to make clear to my French friends. Aramis was easier to manage than his namesake. Meanwhile, our minister was very much troubled over the matter, and the count hardly less so. But Porthos was as inexorable as his namesake, and Merton merely obstinate. It was what the count described as an *impasse*.

VIII

AT this time the Emperor—for this was in the fall of '62—was busy about his Mexican venture, and our legations were disturbed by vague rumors of efforts to combine the great powers in an agreement to bring about a perilous intervention in our affairs, which at home were going badly enough, with one disaster after another. No one at the legation knew how deep the Emperor was in the matter, but there was a chill of expectation in the air, and yet no distinct evidence of the trouble which was brewing.

It was, as I have said, an essential part of my work to frequent the best houses and in every way to learn what was the tone of feeling. It was, in fact, so hostile that it was now and then hard to avoid personal quarrels. In England it was, if possible, worse. Mr. Gladstone had spoken in public, and with warm praise of Mr. Jefferson Davis and the confederation. Roebuck had described our army as the "scum of Europe." We had few important friends in England or France. The English premier was, to say the least, unfriendly, and Lord John Russell in their Foreign Office was not much better.

Meanwhile I came to know and like the Count le Moyne, who was a warm Napoleonist, and whom I had to see often, either on our impossible duel or on diplomatic business. During this familiar intercourse, I began to notice that he was distracted and, I thought, worried.

When I spoke of it to Merton, he said, "That 's the woman." He had no reason to think so, but he was one of the rare men whose intuitions are apt to be correct. This business of the duel went on for a week.

To go back a little, I should have said
that at the end of his two days' leave Alphonse appeared and asked for three days
more. He had no report to make, and went
away again.

On the next day but one I was writing
letters in my salon, and Merton was growl-
ing over the unpleasant news our papers
were bringing us. Suddenly Alphonse appeared. He waited without a word until I
said, "You have found her."

"Yes; it was all that there is of simple.
Monsieur had said she is an American—I
went to the American church."

Merton looked at me, smiling, as he remarked, "Like all the great things, it was
simple."

"I saw the lady come out after the morning service. When I began to follow her at a
distance I saw that she was also followed by
one of the best men of the police. I know
him well. I also perceived that, as it seemed

to me, the lady was uneasy, and, I think, aware that she was watched."

Here Merton stopped him. "You are sure that is the same woman you saw in the carriage."

"Monsieur, when once this lady has been seen, she is not to be forgotten."

"Ha!" exclaimed the captain; "I told you so, Greville. But go on, Alphonse."

"And cut it short," said I, impatient.

Alphonse paused. "Circumstances, monsieur, oblige me to speak in some detail. I was two years in the service. Those who watch and follow madame are of the best. I know them. Therefore there is something serious."

"And her name?" I asked.

"Mme. Bellegarde, Rue de St. Victor, No. 31—a small private hôtel. I regret not to be able to report more fully, but I am well known as monsieur's valet. To appear too curious would be unwise."

[78]

I regarded my valet with increasing respect, while Merton ejaculated, "Damn such a country!" and I asked:

"Is that all?"

"Yes, monsieur; but circumstances—"

"Oh, that will do," I said. "You may go."

When alone with Merton, he said to me, "You must call on her."

"No," I said; "she is suspected of something and I, at least for a time, was taken to be an accomplice. That would never do."

"You are right," returned Merton, thoughtfully; "quite right. You must keep quiet. The matter, whatever it may be, is still unsettled; but I am resolute to find what this woman has done, and why she is watched like a suspected thief. I never was more curious."

For a moment we considered the situation in silence. At last Merton said, "If this woman goes out into society, might you not chance to meet her?"

"Yes, but I never as yet have done so, and I remember faces well. I may meet her any day, or never meet her at all, but any direct approach we must give up. The more I think of it, the graver it appears. If it be a police affair, no letter reaches her unopened. Rest assured of that. She is like a fly in a cobweb. Chance may help us, but so far the luck has been against us."

"No," said Merton; "the game is not played out. There is something they don't know, and they are, therefore, no better off than we."

With this he went away and Alphonse returned. The man was plainly troubled. He said he could do no more, and that when he had made his report to the police that day he had been told to keep a closer watch on me and my letters. Might he show them a note or two?

I said, laughing: "Yes; there are two replies to invitations and a note to my tailor."

That would do, and might he venture to say that monsieur would be well advised to keep out of the matter?

I thanked him, and there the thing stood over for several days longer.

IX

TWO days later I dined at one of the great Bonapartist houses. I was late, and as the guests were about to go to dinner, our hostess said, "Let me present you to a fellow countrywoman, M. Greville of the American Legation—Mme. Bellegarde." I was so taken aback that I could hardly find words to speak to her until we sat down together at dinner. She, too, was equally agitated. I talked awhile to my left-hand neighbor, but presently her adjoining table companion spoke to her and being thus set free, I said to Mme. Bellegarde in English, speaking low:

"You are my countrywoman, and are, as I know, in trouble. What is it? After we met I learned your name, but I have been prudent enough to refrain from calling."

She said: "Yes; you are right. I am in trouble, and of my own making. In my distress that awful night I did not want to give my name to a stranger, and now to recognize in my companion one of our own legation is really a piece of great good fortune. We cannot talk here. I may be able to be of service to the legation—to my country, but we dare not talk here. What I have to say is long. You must not call on me, but we must meet. Come to the masked ball at the palace to-morrow—no, not you. Some one who is not of the legation—some one you can trust. It is a masquerade as you must know. I shall wear a mask—a black domino with a red rose on one sleeve, a white one on the other. Let your friend say, 'Lincoln.' I shall answer, 'America." But do let him be careful."

I said, "Yes; I will arrange it."

[83]

"Oh, thank you. Talk now of something else."

I said, "Yes, in a moment." It occurred to me that I might use Merton. "My friend will be in our army uniform, an entirely unsuspected man. How pretty those flowers are!"

I found her charming, a widow, and if I might judge from her jewels, one at ease in regard to money. Before we left, after dinner, I had a few minutes more of talk with her in the drawing-room. She was free from the look of care I had observed when presented.

"Good-by," I said, as we parted, "and be assured that you have friends."

"Oh, thank you!" she murmured. "But I am involving others in my difficulties. I wish I had never done it. Good night." I went home, curious and perplexed.

Early in the morning of the next day I went to the rooms of our first secretary. In reply to my request, he said he had two cards for the ball at my disposal, and would arrange matters with the master of ceremonies. I accepted one card for Merton, and went away well pleased and regretful that I found it better, as she had done, to leave this singular errand to another.

I made haste to call on Merton, and finding him in, related my fortunate meeting with Mme. Bellegarde, and told him what she expected us to do. He was much pleased, and I happy in finding for our purpose a man whom no one was likely to watch. I urged him, however, to be cautious, and went away, arranging that he should call on me after the ball, even though his visit might be far on in the night. I was too curious and too anxious to wait longer.

It was after three in the morning when he aroused me from the nap into which I had fallen.

"By George!" he cried, "she is a delightful and a brave woman. I told you so; but, good heavens! she is in a sad scrape."

"Well, what is it? Has she robbed the Bank of France?"

"Worse. I told you it was some diplomatic tangle. I was right. It is a big one."

"For Heaven's sake, go on!"

"She is beautiful."

"Of course; I know that. But what happened?"

"I said she was beautiful."

"Yes, twice, and you have never seen her face."

"No, but you told me so. However, I went early and waited about the door until she came in. I kept her in sight. It was n't easy. A half-hour later I got my chance. She had been left by her last partner near a small picture-gallery, and was chatting with an old lady. I said, 'It is my dance, I believe.' She rose at once. As we moved away I whispered, 'Lincoln,' and on her replying, 'America,' she guided me through the gallery and at last into a small conservatory and behind some orange-trees. No one was near. 'One moment,' she said; 'even here I am not free.' I saw no evidence of her being watched, but she was, I fancied, in an agony of apprehension. As I mentioned my name and tried to reassure her, she let fall her black domino saying, 'Quick, push it under that sofa!' She wore beneath it a pearl-colored silk domino, and, of course, was still masked."

"By George!" said I, "a woman of resources. How clever that was!"

Merton went on: "Then we sat down, I saying: 'Be cool, and don't hurry. You are entirely secure.' She did go on, and what a story! She said:

" 'On .the night before I involved Mr Greville in trouble, I went to an evening party at Count le Moyne's. I was never there before, or only to call on the countess, and at that time talked a few minutes with the count. They have been here hardly more than a month. When I arrived there was a great crush in the hall and on the stair. As I waited to get rid of my wraps the count came through the crowd and passed me. He had, I suppose, been belated at the Foreign Office. He seemed to be in haste and went behind a screen and into a room on the side of the hall. A little later the music upstairs ceased. I heard cries of fire. People rushed down the stairway screaming. There was a jam in the hall and a terrible crush at the outer doors. A curtain had been blown across a console and taken fire; that was all, but the alarm and confusion were dreadful. Women fainted. One or two men made brutal efforts to escape. I have a temperament which leaves me pretty cool in real danger. There was none but what the terror of these people created. I was hustled about and, with others, driven against the Chinese screen which covered the doorway of the count's office. I said he had entered it—yes, I told you that. As the alarm grew, it must have reached him, for he came out and had to use violence to push the screen away so as to let him pass. The tumult was at its height as he went by me crying, '*Mon Dieu!*' He ran along a back passageway and disappeared. There were other women near, but I was so placed as to be able to slip behind the screen he had pushed away. I am afraid that he recognized me. As I thus took refuge in the doorway the screen was crushed against it, and I was caught. Of course I was excited, but I was cool compared with the people outside. I tried the door behind me and felt it open. Then I saw that I was in the count's private office. On the table a lamp was burning. As I was crossing the room to try a side-door entrance into the garden, I caught sight of a large paper en-

velop on the table. I could not help seeing
the largely written inscription. I paused.
In an instant I realized that I was in an
enemy's country and had a quick sense of
anger as I read: *"Foreign Office. Confidential. Recognition of the Confederate States.
Note remarks by his Majesty the Emperor.
Make full digest at once. Haste required!
Drouyn de Lhuys."* I stood still. For a
moment, believe me, I forgot the fire—everything. I suppose the devil was at my side.'

" 'A good devil,' said I.

"She said: 'Oh, please not to laugh. It
was terrible. If you had lived in France
these two years you would know. I have
been all summer in the utmost distress about
my country. I have been insulted and
mocked because of our failures. Women can
be very cruel. The desirability of France
and England acknowledging the Confederacy was almost daily matter of talk among
the people I met. Here before me, in my

power, was information sure to be valuable to our legation—to my country. I little dreamed of its importance. I did not reflect. I acted on impulse. I seized the big envelop and drew my cloak around me. The package was bulky and heavy.' "

"Good heavens! ·Merton," said I, "She stole it!"

"Stole it! Nonsense! It was war—glorious."

I shook my head in disapproval, and had at once a vast longing to see our worried and anxious envoys profit by the beautiful thief's outrageous robbery.

Merton continued: "I will go on to state it as well as I can in her own words. She said: 'I stood a moment in doubt, but the noise in the hall increased. The screen was driven in fragments against the door. I might be caught at any moment. That would mean ruin. I tried the side door. It was not locked, and in a moment I found myself outside, in the garden. I went around to the front of the house, and in a minute or two secured a cabriolet and was driven home. Then my worst troubles began. I had acted on impulse. It was wrong. I was a thief. Was it not wrong? Oh, I know it was wicked! To think, sir, that I should have done such a thing!'

"When she spoke out in this way," said Merton, "I saw that if we were to help her, it was essential that we should know whether she was becoming irresolute. To test her I said: 'But, madame, you could have given it back to the count next day. You may be sure he would never have told; and now, poor man, he is in a terrible scrape, and that unlucky Foreign Office! It is not yet too late. Why not return the papers?"

"For a moment I felt ashamed, because even before I made this effort to see if it was worth while to take the grave risks which I saw before us, I knew that she was sobbing."

"It was worth while. But what," I asked, "did she say?" If Merton had said that she was weakening, I should have felt some relief and more disappointment.

He asked in turn, "What do you think she said?"

For my part, I could only reply that it was a question of character, but that while she might feel regret and express her penitence in words, a woman who had done what she had done would never express it in acts.

Merton said, "Thank you," which seemed to me a rather odd reply. He rose as he spoke and for a moment walked about in silence, and then said: "By George! Greville, I felt as if I had insulted her. You think I was right—it is quite a relief." He spoke with an amount of emotion which appeared to me uncalled for.

"Yes, of course you were right; but what did she say?"

" 'Say?' She said: 'I am not a child, sir.

I did what I know to be wrong. I did it
for no personal advantage. I am punished
when I think of myself as a thief. I have
already suffered otherwise. I do not care.
I did it for my country, as—as you kill men
for it. I shall abide by what I did and may
God forgive me! But if you are ashamed—
if you are shocked—if you think—oh, if
you fear to assist me, you will at least consider what I have said as a confidence.' She
stood up as she answered me, and spoke out
with entire absence of care about being over-
heard. Ah, but I wanted to see that masked
face! I said twice as she spoke: 'Be
careful. You mistake me.' She took not
the least notice of my caution. Then at
last I said: 'Pray sit down. It was—it is
clear, madame, that all concerned or who
may concern themselves, with this matter
must feel absolute security that there will be
no weakness anywhere. After what you
have said, and with entire trust in you, we

shall at all risks see this thing through.'
She said, 'Thank you,' and did sit down.

"Then I went on: 'I want to ask you a
question or two. Did the count recognize
you?'

" 'I was not sure at the time, but he must
have at least suspected me, for he called next
day at an unusually early hour, insisted on
seeing me, and frankly told me that on the
night before, during the fire, a document had
been stolen from his table. He had remembered me as near to the office. Did I know
anything about it? I said, "How could I?" I
was dreadfully scared, but I replied that I
had certainly gone through his office and had
left both doors open. Then he said, "It is
too grave a matter for equivocation, and I
ask, Did you take it?" I said I was insulted,
and upon this he lost his temper and threat-
ened all manner of consequences.'

X

"TO cut it short, Greville, she refused to be questioned, and, I fancy, lied rather more plainly than she was willing to admit to me. He went away furious and reasonably sure, or so I think, that she had the papers."

"I see," said I. "He had been careless. Of course, he hesitated for a day or two to confess his loss. But what about those papers? Where are they? She ought to have taken them at once to the legation."

"Yes, but that is easily explained. The count called early, and after that she felt sure that she would be promptly arrested. He was too ashamed to go at once to any such length. He must be an indecisive man. At all events, he took no positive action until after our encounter and her escape, when he

became still more sure where she was going
and why. You see, he lacked the good sense
to confess instantly to the head of his office.
Arrest would have been instantaneous. He
waited, ashamed to confess, and I presume
did not fully inform the police he called in.
Now, I suppose, he has had to confess his
loss to his superiors."

"But these papers?" said I.

"Well, don't hurry me. When she got
home that night and read the papers she had
—well, taken, she saw their enormous value
to our government. Their importance increased her alarm, and the count's visit added
to her sense of need to conceal somewhere
the proofs of her guilt. After her first
fatal delay of the next morning, she was
afraid to carry the papers to the legation.
She could trust no one. She believed the
Emperor's minister would act at once. She
knew that, soon or late, her town house
would be searched. To keep the papers

about her would not do. She must hide
them at once, and then we must hear of them;
and no letters would serve her purpose. She
was panic-stricken. I fancy the count, having been careless, was as anxious, but told no
one that day. This gave her a chance until
luck played her a trick. The count's interview in the morning, while it frightened her,
had not helped him. The next day his superiors would have to be told, and I have no
doubt have been.

"Then, as you know, it came his turn to
have a bit of good fortune. Walking in
haste to escape a ducking, he must have
turned into the Rue du Roi de Rome to get
a cab, and was just in time to see her enter
your carriage. Very likely he did not see
you at all. Indeed, we may be sure that he
did not. When, too, the count saw that, in
place of turning homeward, she was being
driven toward the Bois, his suspicions were
at once aroused. I ought to say that, to

avoid using her own carriage, she had set
out to walk. She was not yet watched,
though she may have thought she was, and
her plan was a good one. Curious and
troubled, he caught a cabriolet and followed,
as was natural enough.

"The direction of your flight through the
Bois confirmed his suspicions. He may have
guessed, and he was right, that she was about
to go to her well-known little country house
and meant to hide the papers. I am trying
to follow what must have been his course of
thought and would have been mine. He
would catch her and get them, even at the
cost of arresting her. So far this is in part
her account and in part my inferences. As
we talked thus at length, she was again in-
describably uneasy and took every one who
passed for a spy."

"Well," said I, "I do not wonder. The
court is cool to us. Something hostile to our
country is going on between France and

England. The English abuse is exhausting their adjectives. If they propose intervention in any shape, Mr. Adams has instructions of which every American should be proud."

"Good!" cried Merton. "We have not put forth our power, and people over here do not dream of the way in which we could and would rise to meet new foes. But here is our own little battle. I have yet to tell you what she did and my further reflections. After you got her away from the count, and Alphonse guided her, she walked through the rain in the darkness to her small chalet beyond the Bois.

"But," said I, "why did not the count follow and get there, as he could have done, before her?"

"I do not know. He was, you said, a bit dazed and his head cut. Probably he felt it to be needful to secure aid from the police, as he did later."

"Yes, that must have been the case."

"Her old American nurse has charge of the chalet. At times madame spends a few days there. She explained her condition as the result of a carriage accident, and, I fancy, must have taken her nurse into her confidence. She did not tell me. A fire was made in her boudoir, and, with some change of dress, she sat down to think. She knew that, soon or late, the count must confess his loss, and then that the whole police force of Paris would concentrate its skill first on preventing her from using the papers, and finally on securing them. They would at once suspect that she had made her singular dash for the chalet to conceal the papers, as the count must have inferred. She was one woman against the power, intelligence, and limitless resources of an army. If the count acted with reasonable promptness, the time left her to hide the papers was likely to be short.

"She had adopted and dropped one plan after another as she walked through the night. Then, as she sat in despair, she had an inspiration. The fireplace was kept, after the common American way, full of un-removed wood ashes. It suggested a re-source. To lessen the size of the package she hastily removed the many envelops of the contained papers and also the thick double outside cover. Then she tied them together, raked away the newly made fire, and setting the lessened package on the hearth, far back, piled the cold ashes over it. It was safe from combustion. Finally, she replaced the cinders and set on top some burning twigs and a small log or two. The fire was soon burning brightly. For a few minutes she sat thinking that she must burn the envelops. It was now late. The gate-bell rang. Three hours had gone by since she left the count. In great haste she tore up the thick outside envelops and other covers and hastily scattered them on the flames. She did succeed in burning the larger part of the covers, and only by accident, or rather by reason of her haste, was, as I shall tell you, lucky enough to leave unburned a bit of the outer cover. However, she piled on more twigs, and had settled herself by the fire when her nurse entered in company with a man in civilian dress and two of the police. They used little ceremony and said simply that she was believed to have certain papers. Best to give them up and save trouble. Of course, she denied the charge and was indignant. Then they made a very complete search, after which two of them remained with her, and the other, leaving, came back in an hour with a woman who went with her to her room and there made a very rigorous personal search of her own and her nurse's garments. She, of course, protested vigorously. At last, returning to her boudoir, she found the man in civilian dress kneeling beside the fire. She was in an agony of alarm. The man had gathered the fragments of half-burned paper, and when she entered was staring at the unconsumed corner of the outer official envelop. Without a word, he raked away the fire and a part of the ashes, but seeing there no evidence of interest, contented himself with what proof he had of the destruction of the documents he sought. The appearance of much burned paper and the brightly blazing fire, I suppose, helped to confirm his belief. To her angry protests he replied civilly that it was a matter for his superiors. Finally, an officer was left in charge, but she was allowed to send for a carriage and to return home. It is clear that they are not satisfied, and the house has been watched ever since. Of course, the man who found the charred fragments of the official envelop concluded that she had burned the contents. But some one else who knows their value will doubt."

"I suppose so. They were less clever than usual."

"No; her haste saved her. The unburned corner of the envelop fooled the man. How could he dream that under a hot fire, cool and safe, were papers worth a fortune?"

"Certainly this time the luck is hers," said I; "but this will not satisfy them."

"No. More than once since they have been over the house and garden and utterly devastated it, so says her nurse. They searched a tool-house and a small conservatory. Madame Bellegarde has been cool enough to go there for flowers, but is in the utmost apprehension. And now ten days have passed."

"Is that all?"

"No. She has been questioned pretty brutally over and over, but as yet they have not searched her town house. They are sure that the papers are in the villa."

"Well, what next?" I asked.

"She says we must get those papers. That is our business."

"It will be difficult," I returned; "and there should be no delay. It must be done, and done soon. You or I would have found her cache."

"No, I should not; but if those people are still in doubt, as seems to be the case, and decide that no one but a fool would have burned the documents, some fellow with a little more imaginative capacity to put himself in her place will find them."

"By the way," added Merton, "she described the house to me. Now let us think it over. I shall be here at nine to-morrow morning. When I return, you will give me your own thoughts about it. Given a house already watched day and night, how to get a paper out of it? No one will be allowed to leave it without being overhauled. The old nurse, you may be sure, will be searched and followed, even when she goes to market. To communicate with madame would not be easy, and would give us no further help and only hurt her. It is so grave a matter that the police, after another search, will arrest Mme. Bellegarde secretly and, if possible, scare her into confession. We have no time to lose. It must be done, too, in some simple way. For her sake we must avoid violence, and whatever is done must be done by us."

"But, Merton, how can we get into the house, even if we enter the garden unseen?"

"Oh, I forgot to say that she has said she would contrive to tell her nurse to leave the conservatory unlocked, and also the door between it and the house. I told you she has been there twice. On each occasion she was watched, but was allowed to enter and pick flowers. She feels sure of being able to warn the nurse. We must give her a day. But why do they not arrest her? That would have been my first move."

I replied: "Her late husband's people are

Bonapartists and very influential. It would have to be explained, and the situation is an awkward one. The mere destruction of the papers is not what they most desire; neither do they want the loss known, and very likely they desire to conceal it as long as possible from the Emperor. I have been unable to think of any plan. Has the night left you any wiser?"

' "I? Yes, indeed. I have a plan—a good one and simple. When I was a boy and coveted apples, one fellow got over the fence and attracted the attention of the farmer, while the other secured apples in a far corner of the orchard. Don't you see?"

"No, I do not."

"Well, it is simple. Just see how easy it is. We attract the attention of the guards, and then one of us goes into the house."

"But," said I, "if he meets there a resolute guard."

"And if," said Merton, "the guard is met

by a more resolute man, let us say, with a revolver."

"Merton, it is a thing to be done without violence."

"Or not at all?" queried Merton, with what I may call an examining glance.

"No, I did not say that."

The captain, I suppose, understood my state of mind, for he said: "I feel as you do. You are quite right; but if it becomes needful to use positive means,—I say positive means to get these papers,—then—" I shook my head and he went on, "You may rest assured that I shall use no violence unless I am obliged to do so."

"You will have no chance," said I, "because I, as a member of the legation, must be the one to enter the house. No one else should. You may readily see why."

Merton was disappointed, and in fact said so, while admitting that I was in the right. He looked grave as he added: "We are playing a game, you and I, in which, quite possibly, the fate of our country is involved, and, also, the character and fate of a woman. If we win, no one can convict her of having taken these papers. On their side there will be no hesitation. There should be none on ours."

I said nothing to relieve his evident doubt as to the spirit with which I had undertaken a perilous venture. I, on my part, simply insisted that the larger risk must be mine. He finally assented with a laugh, saying he was sorry to miss the fun of it. After some careful consideration of his plan and of our respective shares in carrying it out, he went away, leaving me to my reflections. They would, I presume, have amused and surprised the man who had just left me. I had led a quiet, studious life, and never once had I been where it was requisite to face great danger or possible death. I had often wondered whether I possessed the form of courage which makes certain men more competent, the greater the peril. As I sat I confessed to myself an entire absence of the joy in risks with which Merton faced our venture, but at the same time I knew that I was not sorry for a chance to satisfy myself in regard to an untested side of my own character. I knew, too, that I should be afraid, but would that lessen my competence? I had a keen interest in the matter, and was well aware that there was very real danger and possible disgrace if we were caught in a position which we could not afford to explain.

XI

ON the following morning I was at breakfast, when Alphonse said to me: "I made last night sir, pretense of following monsieur, and discovered that another man was doing the same thing. Circumstances permitted me to observe that he was stupid, but monsieur will perceive that either I am mistrusted by the police, or that the affair of madame is growing more difficult and has so far baffled the detectives. The count must have mentioned your name to them." There he paused and busied himself with the coffee-urn, and, for my part, I sat still, wondering whether I had not better be more entirely frank with this unusual valet. He knew enough to be very dangerous, and now stood at ease, evidently expecting some comment on my part. I had asked Merton to breakfast, and a half-hour later he came in, apologizing and laughing.

"Well," he said, "I am late. I had Lieutenant West to see me, and, to my grief, Aramis is out of it and has explained, and so on; but Porthos is inexorable. I said at last I was so tired of them all that I should accept rapiers if the big man would give me time. The fact is, we must first dispose of this other business. A wound, or what not, might cripple me. I am not a bad hand with the sword, and I take lessons twice a day. But now about the other affair. This duel is a trifle to it."

Alphonse had meanwhile gone, at a word from me, and I was free to open my mind to Merton. He did not hesitate a moment. "Call him back," he said, "and let me talk to him."

Alphonse reappeared.

"I gave you three hundred francs," said Merton.

"Yes, monsieur."

"Where is it?"

"My mother has it."

"Very good. Are you for the emperor?"

The man's face changed. "M. le Capitaine knows that a man must live. I was of the police, but my father was shot in the coup d'état. I am a republican."

"If so," said Merton, "for what amount would you sell your republican body and soul?"

"As to my body, monsieur, that is for sale cheap."

"And souls are not dear in France," said Merton.

"Yes, monsieur; but the price varies."

"What would you say to—well, a thousand francs down and a thousand in three months?"

"If monsieur would explain."

I did not dislike his caution, but I still had a residue of doubt as to the man who was serving two masters. Merton had none. He went on:

"We mean to be plain with you. We are caught in the net of a big and dangerous business."

"I had thought as much," said Alphonse. "Would M. le Capitaine explain? No doubt there are circumstances—"

"Precisely. A woman has done what makes it necessary for us to recover a certain document despite the police and the government. Understand that if we succeed you get two thousand francs and run meanwhile risks of a very serious nature."

"And my master?"

"Oh, he may lose his position. You and I and madame may be worse off."

"As to my position," I said, "leave me out of the question. We shall all take risks."

"Then I accept," said Alphonse. "Monsieur has been most kind to my mother, and circumstances have always attracted me—

monsieur will understand. What am I to do?"

"You are to examine the outside of Madame Bellegarde's villa by day and at night—to-night—and report to us to-morrow morning. I have a scheme for entering it and securing the document we want, but of that we will speak when we hear your report. I have already ridden around the place. I am trusting you entirely."

"No, monsieur, not quite entirely," said Alphonse, smiling.

Merton understood this queer fellow as I did not, for, as I sat wondering what he meant, my friend said quietly: "No we have not told you where the papers are concealed nor what they are. And you want to know?"

A sudden panic seemed to fall on the valet. He winked rapidly, looked to right and left, and then cried in a decisive way, with open hands upraised as if to push away something: "No, monsieur, no. Circumstances make it not to be desired."

From that moment I trusted the man. "Is that all, monsieur?" he said.

"No. I do not want you to act without knowing that we, all of us, are about to undertake what is against the law and may bring death or, to you at least, the galleys."

"I accept." He said it very quietly. "What other directions has monsieur, or am I merely to report about the house and the guards? It is easy."

"Yes, that is all at present. The danger comes later. Let us hear at nine to-morrow morning."

His report at that time was clear and not very reassuring. There were guards at or near the gateway. At night a patrol moved at times around the outside. He saw a man enter the garden and remain within. He could not say whether there was another one

in the house. It was likely. Madame Bellegarde had driven to the villa. She had been
allowed to enter, and came out with a basket
of flowers. As no one went in with her, it
was pretty sure that they trusted some one
within to watch her.

Merton said: "And now, Alphonse, have
you any plan, any means by which we can
enter that house at night and get away safe
without violent methods?"

"If there was no one within."

"But we do not know, and that we must
risk."

"It would be necessary," said Alphonse,
"to get the police away from the gate for
a time, and, if I am not mistaken, their
orders will be capture, dead or alive. They
believe your papers are still hidden in that
house and that an effort may be made to secure them. You observe, monsieur, that all
this care would never be taken in an ordinary case. If monsieur proposes to enter the

house and take away certain papers, the guard may resist, and in that case—"

"In that case," laughed Merton, "circumstances—"

"Monsieur does not desire me to enter the house."

I said promptly that we did not. Alphonse seemed relieved, and Merton went on to state with care his own plan. Alphonse listened with the joy of an expert, adding suggestions and twice making very good comments on our arrangements. It would be necessary he thought, to wait for a stormy night, but already it was overclouded.

Alphonse went away to see his mother and to make his own preparations for the share assigned to him in an adventure to which I looked forward with keen interest and with small satisfaction.

Not so Merton. When the valet left us, the captain said: "We are utterly in the hands of that man."

"Yes," I returned thoughtfully.

"If he knew," said Merton, "he might—"

"No. That he did not want to know what these papers are was an expression of his own doubt concerning the extent to which he might trust himself. I think we must trust him."

"Yes," returned the captain. "Whether or not we have been wise to use him, I rather doubted, but now I do not. The limitations of the moral code of a man like Alphonse are strange enough. It is hard to guess beforehand what he will do and what he will not. However, we are in for it. You have a revolver?"

"No."

"I will lend you mine."

I said I should be glad to borrow it, but I may say that I took care, before we set out, to see that the barrels were not loaded. I might use it to threaten, but was resolute not to fire on any one, even if not to do so involved failure of our purpose. I, too, had my moral limitations.

We lost a day, but on the following night there was such a storm as satisfied us to the full.

XII

ABOUT eight o'clock we drove to a little restaurant in the Bois de Boulogne, dined quietly, and about nine set out on foot to walk to the villa. There was a brief lull in the storm, but very soon the rain fell again heavily, and as, of course, we took no umbrellas, we were soon wet to the skin.

Making sure that we were not followed, we approached the garden cautiously through the wood, the rain falling in torrents. At the edge of the forest, near a well known fountain, beyond the house, we met by appointment my man, Alphonse. He was dressed as an old woman and had an empty basket on his arm. Together we moved through the wood and shrubbery until we were opposite the side of the garden and about a hundred feet from where the wall turned at a right angle.

Here, facing an avenue, the wall was broken midway by the arch of the entrance gateway. The wind blew toward us, and we could hear now and then the sound of voices.

Alphonse said: "Two; there are two at the gate."

"Hush," said I, as a man came around the angle and along the narrow way between us and the garden wall.

"Wait, monsieur; he will come again." In some ten minutes he reappeared, as before.

"Now," said Merton, and in a pour of wildly driven rain Alphonse disappeared. He found his way through the wood and in to the main avenue, which in front of the gate turned to the left and passed around the farther side of the grounds. Then he walked up to the gate. Before long we

heard words of complaint. Would the
guards tell her— This was all gleefully related afterward. She had lost her way.
Yes, a little glass of absinthe—only one.
She was not used to it. And she had the
money for her market sales, and alas! so
she was all wrong and must go back. The
guards laughed. No doubt it was the absinthe. The old woman was reeling now and
then. Would n't one of them show her the
way? No. And was it down the avenue?
Yes. With this she set off unsteadily along
the road to the left. They called out that it
was the wrong way, and then, laughing, dismissed her.

When once around the remote angle of
the wall, Alphonse slipped aside into the
forest, got rid of gown and basket, and
moving through the wood, took up his station on the side of the main avenue of approach to the villa, and out of sight of the
guards. Here he waited until a few minutes
later he was joined by the captain.

Meanwhile I stood in the wood with Merton. I think he enjoyed it. I did not. A first attempt at burglary is not in all its aspects heroic, and I was wet, chilled, and anxious.

"First actor on," murmured Merton. "Should like to have seen that interview. Can't be actor and audience both."

I hazily reflected that for myself I was both, and that the actor had just then a sharp fit of stage-scare. I let him run on unanswered, while the rain poured down my back.

At last he said: "I think Alphonse has had time enough."

"Hardly," said I. I did not want to talk. I was longing to do something—to begin. The punctual guard went by twenty feet away, the smoke of his pipe blown toward us.

"I never liked pipe-smoking on the picket-line," said Merton. "You can smell it of a damp night at any distance. Remind me to tell you a story about it. Heavens!" he cried, as a flash of lighting for an instant set everything in noon-day clearness, "I hope we shall not have much of that. Keep down, Greville. Ever steal apples? Strike that repeater." I did so. "It's a good deal like waiting for the word to charge. I remember that once we labeled ourselves for recognition in case we did not come out alive. Just after that I fell ill."

"Hush!" I said. "There he is again."

"All right; give him a moment," said Merton, "and now you have a full half-hour. Come."

We crossed the narrow road and stood below the garden wall. He gave me the aid of his bent knee and then his shoulder, and I was at once lying flat on the garden wall. My repeater rang 10:15, and then, as I lay, I heard voices. This time there were two men. They paused on the road just below me to light cigarettes. One of them consigned the weather to a place where it might have proved more agreeable. The other said Jean had a pleasanter station in the house. This was not very reassuring news, but I was in for it and wildly eager to be through with a perilous adventure.

As they disappeared, I dropped from the wall into the garden and fell with an alarming crash, rolling over on a pile of flowerpots. There was such a clatter as on any quiet night must have been surely heard. For a moment I lay still, and then, hearing no signals of alarm, I rose and groped along the wall to the door of the conservatory. It was not locked. Pausing on the step outside for a moment, I took off my shoes and secured them by tying them to a belt I wore for this purpose. Then I went in. I found the door of the house ajar, and entering, knew that I was in the drawing-room. I moved with care, in the gloom, through the furniture, and, aided by a flash of light-

ning, found my way into the hall. Before
me, to left, across the hall, was a small room.
The door was open. I smelled very vile pipe-
smoke and heard footfalls overhead, but
no sound of voices. I became at once hope-
ful that I should have to deal with but one
man. I opened cautiously a window in the
little room and sat down to listen and wait.
I had been given a half-hour. My repeater
at last struck 10:45. Meanwhile the clouds
broke in places, and there were now gleams
of unwelcome moonlight and now gusts of
wind-driven rain.

I rose and shut to a crack the door of the
room and waited. Beyond the wall, to my
right, I heard of a sudden a wild shriek of
"Murder! murder! Help! help!" shrill, fem-
inine, convincing. Then came a pistol-shot,
then another, and in a moment a third more
remote, and, far away, the cries of men.

My time had come. That the gate guards
would make for the direction of the sound

we had felt sure, but what would happen in regard to the house guard was left to chance. At all events, he would be isolated for a time. To my relief, the ruse answered. I shut the window noiselessly as I heard my host running down the stairway.

He opened the hall door in haste and was dimly seen from my window hurrying toward the gate. I rushed into the hall, bolted the hall door, and ran up-stairs. The old nurse had been prepared for my coming and met me on the first landing.

"Quick," I said. "You expected me. The boudoir." She had her good Yankee wits about her, and in a minute I was kneeling, wildly anxious, and groping in the ashes. Thrusting the package of paper within my shirt-bosom, I ran down-stairs, and as she came after, I cried that I had locked the hall door, and to unlock it when I was gone. "Be quick," I added, "and lock the conservatory door behind me. No one has been seen by you. Go to your own room." Pausing to put on my shoes, I fled across the garden, neither hearing nor seeing the guard who must have joined his fellows outside.

XIII

I HAD an awful five minutes in my efforts
to climb the wall. We had forgotten that.
For a minute I was in despair, and then I
fell over a garden chair. I dragged it to
the wall and somehow scrambled up, and,
panting, lay still for a moment, listening.
I suppose that, becoming suspicious, they
had returned, for two of the men passed by
below me, talking fast, and if they had
been less busy over the pistol-shots and had
merely looked up from a few feet away, I
should have been caught. I waited, breath-
ing. hard A few minutes passed. They seemed
to be hours. The noises ceased. I saw dimly
through the torrents of rain my house guard
returning to his post. He went in, and at

once I turned over, dropped, and in a moment
was deep in the wood. I was drenched and
as tired of a sudden as if I had walked all
day. I suppose it was due to the intense
anxiety and excitement of my adventure. I
went on for a half-mile, keeping my hand
on the package. It was now after eleven,
and I sat down in the wood and rested for a
while. I knew Paris well. I had been there
two years. I walked on for nearly an hour,
and then within one of the barriers, remote
from the Bois, I caught a cab and drove to
the Rue Rivoli, where I left the man and
walked to our legation in the Rue de Pres-
bourg. We kept there a night-watchman,
and both he and the concierge must have
been amazed at my appearance. I went up
to my own room, had a roaring fire kindled,
locked the door, found a smoking-jacket,
and then, with a glass of good rye and a
cigar, sat down, feeling a delightful sense of
joy and security. Next I turned to exam-

ine the value of my prize. The ashes fell
about as I laid the packet on the table.

I was by degrees becoming warm, and although wet, for I had had no complete
change of garments, I was so elated that I
hardly gave a thought to my condition.
As I sat, the unopened papers before me, I
began to consider, as others have done, the
ethical aspects of the matter. A woman
had stolen the documents now on the table.
To have returned them would have convicted
her. We were on the verge of war with two
great nations. One of them had us in a net
of spies. War, which changes all moral ob-
ligations, was almost on us. I would leave
it to my chief. No more scrupulous gentleman was ever known to me. I undid the
knotted ribbon with which Madame Bellegarde had hastily tied the papers together
and turned to consider them.

My own doubts did, I fear, weaken as,
turning over the documents, I saw revealed

the secrets of my country's enemies. In the
crisis we were facing they were of inestim-
able value. Some of the papers were original letters; others were copies of letters from
the French embassy in London. Among
them was a draft of a letter of Drouyn de
Lhuys, the Minister for Foreign Affairs,
and on this and on others were sharp comments in the emperor's well-known hand,
giving reasons for acknowledging the Confederacy without delay. There were even
hints at intervention by the European
powers as desirable. I sat amazed as at last
I tied up the papers, and placing them again
within my waistcoat, lay down on a lounge
before the fire to rest, for sleep was not for
me. I lay quiet, thinking of what had become of Merton and Alphonse, and wondering at the amazing good fortune of my
first attempt at burglary.

XIV

AT seven in the morning I sent a guarded note to our chief, and at eight he appeared. I need not dwell upon his surprise as he listened to the full relation of my encounter with Le Moyne, about which and our subsequent difficulty he already knew something. When I quietly told him the rest of the story and, untying the ribbon, laid the dusty package on the table, he became grave. He very evidently did not approve of our method of securing the papers, but whatever he may have felt as to the right or wrong of what we had done was lost in astonishment as he saw before him the terribly plain revelation of all we had been so long dreading. Here was the hatching of an international conspiracy. As he sat, his kindly face grew stern while I translated to him the emperor's comments.

"It is evident," he said, "that a résumé of certain of these papers should go to Berlin and Russia in cipher, but this may wait. The originals must as soon as possible reach our minister in London."

While Mr. Dayton considered the several questions involved, the first secretary, who had been sent for, arrived. The minister at once set before him the startling character of the papers on the table, and my story was briefly retold. Upon this there was a long consultation concerning the imminence of the crisis they suggested, and in regard to the necessity of the originals being placed as soon as possible in the hands of Mr. Adams, our able representative at the court of St. James. No one for a moment seemed to consider the documents as other than a lawful prize. We could not burn them. To admit of our having them was to convict

Madame Bellegarde; and not to use them
was almost treason to our country. So
much I gathered from the rapid interchange
of opinions. When the method of sending
them to Mr. Adams came before us, the first
secretary said shrewdly enough:

"If they were sure these papers were in
the villa,—and they were, I fancy,—I wonder they did not accidentally burn the
house."

"That would have been simple and complete," said the chief, smiling, "but there
are original letters here which it was very
desirable to keep, and I presume them to
have felt sure soon or late of recovering
them."

"Yes," said the first secretary, "that is no
doubt true. Now the whole affair is
changed. I am certain that the house will
have been searched and the scattered ashes
seen. They will then feel sure that we have
the papers."

I had to confess that, in my haste, I had taken no pains about restoring the ashes. My footprints in the garden soil and my want of care would help to make plain that the papers had been removed, and any clever detective would then infer what had been the purpose of the pistol-shots. I had been stupid and had to agree with the secretary that they would now know they had been tricked and see that the game so far had been lost. The legation and all of us would be still more closely watched, and I, for one, was also sure that the messenger to England would never see London with the papers still in his possession.

Meanwhile, as the secretary and our chief discussed the question, my mind was on Merton. About ten, to my relief, he sent in his card. He entered smiling.

"Good morning, Mr. Dayton. All right, Greville?"

I said: "Yes, the papers are here,

These gentlemen all know. Had you any trouble?"

"A little. When I fired shot after shot in the air and our man was screaming murder, they all ran toward us like ducks to a decoy. I ran, too, and Alphonse. As I crossed a road, I came upon a big gendarme. I am afraid I hurt him. Oh, not much. After that I had no difficulty. And now perhaps I am in the way." He rose as he spoke.

The minister said: "No. Sit down, captain."

He resumed his seat, and sat a quiet listener to our statement of difficulties. At last he said: "Will you pardon me if I make a suggestion?"

"By all means," said the chief. "It is almost as much your concern as ours."

"I suppose," said Merton, "the despatches to Berlin and St. Petersburg may go in cipher by trusty messengers or any chance tourist, and that there is no need for haste."

"Yes, that is true."

There was a moment's pause in this interesting consultation, the captain evidently waiting to be again invited to state his opinion. At last our chief said: "You have never seen these papers?"

"No, sir."

"Then I had better make clear to you, in strict confidence, that they reveal to us urgent pressure on the part of the emperor to induce England to intervene with France in our sad war. The English cabinet, most fortunately, is not unanimously hostile, and Lord John Russell is hesitating. Our friends are the queen and the great middle class of dissenters, and, strange to say, the Lancashire operatives. The aristocracy, the church, finance, and literature are all our enemies, and at home, you know, things are not altogether as one could wish. Just

now no general, no, not the President, is of
such moment to us as our minister in London. He has looked to us for information.
We could only send back mere echoes of his
own fears. And now"—he struck the pile
of papers with his hand—"here is the whole
story. Mr. Adams must have these without
delay. I should like to see his interview
with Lord John. You seemed to me to have
in mind something further to say. I interrupted only to let you feel the momentous
character of this revelation."

"As I understand it," replied Merton,
"you assume that the Foreign Office here will
be sure these papers are in your hands."

"We may take that for granted. They
are not stupid, and the matter as it stands
is for them, to say the least, awkward."

"Yes, sir, and they will know what a man
of sense should do with these papers and do
at once. I may assume, then, that the whole

resources of the imperial police will be used, and without scruple, to prevent them from leaving Paris or reaching London."

"Yes, said the chief, "of that we may be certain."

"And if now," said Merton, "some one of note, or two persons, go with them to London, there is a fair probability of the man or the papers being—we may say—mislaid, on the way."

"It is possible," said the minister, "quite possible."

"I think, sir," said I, "that is probable, oh, quite certain, and we cannot accept the least risk of their being lost. No copies will answer."

"No. As you all are aware—as we all know, Captain Merton, affairs are at a crisis. The evidence must be complete, past doubt or dispute, such as to enable Mr. Adams to speak decisively—and he will."

"May I, sir," said Merton, "venture to

further suggest that some one, say the first secretary, take a dummy envelop marked 'Important and confidential,' addressed to Mr. Adams, and be not too careful of it while he crosses the Channel?"

"Well," said the minister, smiling, "what next?"

"He will be robbed on the way, or something will happen. It will never get there."

"No. They will stop at nothing," said I.

"I ought to tell you," said the minister, "that now Madame Bellegarde is sure to be arrested" (as in fact did occur). "She will be subject to one of those cruel cross-examinations which are so certain to break down a witness. If this should happen before we can act, they will be so secure of what we shall do that—"

Merton interrupted him. "Excuse me. She will never speak. They will get nothing from her. That is an exceptional woman."

The minister cast a half-smiling glance at

him. He was deeply distressed, as I saw, and added: "You will, I trust, sir, stand by her. They can prove nothing, and she will hold her tongue and resolutely."

"I will do all in my power; rest assured of that. But what next? The papers! Mr. Adams!" He was anxious.

"Might I again venture?"

"Pray do."

"I have or can have an errand in Belgium. Give me the papers. They will reach their destination if I am alive, and, so far, I at least must be entirely unsuspected. My obvious reason for going will leak out and be such as to safeguard my real reason."

"May I ask why you go to Belgium?"

"Yes, I want it known. I have arranged to satisfy a gentleman named Porthos, who thinks himself injured."

"Porthos!" exclaimed the minister. "Why, that is a character in one of Dumas's novels."

"Yes, I beg pardon; we call him Porthos.

Mr. Greville will explain later. He is the Baron la Garde. An absurd affair."

"I deeply regret it," said the minister. "I hoped it was settled. But you may be hurt, and, pardon me, killed."

"In that case my second, Lieutenant West of our navy, will have the papers and carry them to London. Count le Moyne is one of the baron's seconds. He will hardly dream that he is an escort of the papers he lost. But, sir, one word more. Madame Belle-garde is an American. You will not desert her?"

"Not I. Rest easy as to that. We owe her too much."

"Then I am at your service."

"I regret, deeply regret this duel," said our chief, "but it does seem to me, if it must take place, a sure means of effecting our purpose." As he spoke, the secretary gathered up the various papers.

"I think, sir," said Merton, "it will be

well if one, or, better, two responsible people remain here overnight." This seemed to us a proper precaution.

As we had talked I saw Merton playing with the dusty blue ribbon which, when he entered, lay beside the papers. As we rose I missed it, and knew that he had put it in his pocket. After we had arranged for our passports I left with Merton. As we walked away he said:

"I propose that you say at once to the baron's friends that we will leave for Belgium to-morrow. It is not unusual, and I have a right to choose. You must insist. Porthos is wild for a fight, and—confound it, don't look so anxious. This affair has hurried things a little; I wanted more practice. I should be a fool to say I am a match for Porthos, but he is very big. If I can tire him, or get a scratch such as stops these affairs—somehow it will come to an end, and, at all events, how better could I risk my life for my country? It must be lightly talked about in the clubs to-night." West and I took care that it was.

The next day early we were at the legation. The first secretary was preparing the dummy. "Pity," said Merton, "to leave the enclosure a blank." The secretary laughed and wrote on the inside cover:

> Trust you will find this interesting,
> Yours,
>
> *Uncle Sam.*

We went out, Merton and I looking at our passports and talking loudly. At ten that morning the first secretary and an attaché started for London. To anticipate, he was jostled by two men on the Dover pier that afternoon, and until a few minutes later did not detect his loss of the papers. It was cleverly done. Of course he made a complaint and the police proved useless.

XV

THE duel had been duly discussed at the clubs, and it is probable that no one suspected Merton of any other purpose. The baron was eager and Belgium a common resort for duels. On the same day after the secretary's departure for London, Merton took the train for Brussels with Lieutenant West, the baron and his friends, Count le Moyne and the colonel. The captain had the papers fastened under his shirt, and, as I learned later, was well armed. Not the least suspicion was entertained in regard to our double errand, and, as I had talked freely of being one of the seconds, I was able to follow them, as far as I could see, unwatched, except by Alphonse, who promptly reported

me to his other employers as having gone to
Belgium as one of Merton's friends.

In the evening we met Le Moyne and the
little colonel at the small town of Meule,
just over the border, and settled the usual
preliminaries. The next day at 7 A.M. we
met on an open grassy space within a wood.
The lieutenant had the precious papers. We
stepped aside. The word was given and the
blades met. Merton surprised me. It is
needless to enter into details. He was
clearly no match for Porthos, but his wonderful agility and watchful blue eyes served
him well. Then, of a sudden, there was a
quicker contest. The baron's sword entered
Merton's right arm above the elbow. The
seconds ran in to stop the fight, but as the
baron was trying to recover his blade, instead of recoiling, Merton threw himself
forward, keeping the baron's weapon caught
in his arm, and thrust madly, driving his
own sword downward through the baron's

right lung. Then both men staggered back and Porthos fell.

I hurried Merton away to an inn, where the wound his own act had made serious was dressed. Although in much pain, he insisted on our leaving him at once. Lieutenant West and I crossed the Channel that night. At noon next day Mr. Adams had the papers and this queer tale which, as I said, is unaccountably left out of his biography. I have often wondered where, to-day, are those papers.

The count remained with Porthos at a farm-house near by. He made a slow recovery, the colonel complaining bitterly that M. Merton's methods lacked the refinement of the French duel.

The papers contained, among other documents, a rough draft of a letter dated October 15, 1862, from M. Drouyn de Lhuys proposing intervention to the courts of England and Russia. It appeared in the French journals about November 14, when the crisis had passed. Mr. Adams acted on the manly instructions of Mr. Seward, and Mr. Gladstone lived to change his opinions on this matter, as in time he changed almost all his opinions. Madame Bellegarde, unknown to history, had saved the situation. The English minister declined the French proposals.

Soon after I returned, Madame Bellegarde reappeared, and, as soon as he was well enough, Merton went to see her. She had been released, as we supposed she would be, with a promise to say nothing of her examination, and she kept her word. I thought it as well not to call upon her, but when Merton told me of his visit I was malicious enough to ask whether he had returned to her the ribbon. To this he replied that I had a talent for observation and that I had better ask her. She had been ordered to leave France for six months. I am under the impression that he wrote to her and she to him. The thrust in his arm, which would otherwise have been of small moment, his own decisive act had converted into a rather bad open wound, and, as it healed very slowly, under advice he resigned from the army and for a time remained in Paris, where we were much together. In December he left for Italy. I was not surprised to receive in the spring an invitation to the marriage of the two actors in this notable affair. I ought to add that Le Moyne lost his place in the Foreign Office, but, being of an influential family, was later employed in the diplomatic service.

Circumstances, as Alphonse remarked, made it desirable for him to disappear. Merton was additionally generous and my valet married and became the prosperous master of a well-known restaurant in New York.

XVI

LATE in 1868 Merton rejoined the army, and I did not see him again until in 1869, when I was American minister at The Hague. In June of that year Colonel and Mrs. Merton became my guests. When I told Mrs. Merton that Count le Moyne was the French ambassador in Holland, she said to her husband:

"I told you we should meet, and really I should like to tell him how sorry I was for him."

"I fancy," said I, "that the count will hardly think a return to that little corner of history desirable."

"Even," said Merton, laughing, "with the belated consolation of the penitence of successful crime."

"But I am not, I never was penitent. I was only sorry."

"Well," said I, "you will never have the chance to confess your regret."

I was wrong. A week later the countess left cards for my guests, and an invitation to dine followed. If Merton hesitated, Mrs. Merton did not, and expecting to find a large official dinner, we agreed among us that the count had been really generous and that we must all accept. In fact, if Mrs. Merton might be embarrassed by meeting in his own house the man she had so seriously injured, Merton and I were at ease, seeing that we were entirely unknown to the count as having been receivers of the property which so mysteriously disappeared.

We were met by the count and Madame le Moyne with the utmost cordiality. To my surprise, there were no other guests. All of those thus brought together may have felt just enough the awkwardness of the occasion to make them quick to aid one another in dispersing the slight feeling of aloofness natural to a situation unmatched in my social experience.

The two women were delightful, the menu admirable, the wines past praise. It was an artful and agreeable *lever du rideau*, and I knew it for that when, at a word from the count, the servants left us at the close of the meal. Then, smiling, he turned to Mrs. Merton and said:

"Perhaps, madame, you may have understood that in asking you all here and alone I had more than the ordinary pleasant reasons. If in the least degree you object to my saying more, we will consider that I have said nothing, and," he added gaily, "we shall then chat of Rachel and the June exhibition of tulips."

It was neatly done, and Mrs. Merton at once replied: "I wish to say for myself that I have for years desired to talk freely with you of what is no doubt in your mind just now."

"Thank you," he returned; "and if no one else objects,"—and no one did,—"I may say that, apart from my own eager desire to ask you certain questions, my wife has had, for years, what I may call chronic curiosity."

"Oh, at times acute!" cried the countess.

"Her curiosity is, as you must know, in regard to certain matters connected with that mysterious diplomatic affair in the autumn of 1862. It cost me pretty dear."

"And me," said the countess, "many tears."

Mrs. Merton's face became serious. She was about to speak, when the count added: "Pardon me. I am most sincere in my own wish not to embarrass you, our guests, and if, on reflection, you feel that our very natural curiosity ought to die a natural death, we will dismiss the matter. Tell me, would you prefer to drop it?"

"Oh, no. I, too, am curious." And, turning to her husband, "Arthur, I am sure you will be as well pleased as I."

Merton said: "I am entirely at your service, count. How is it, Greville?"

"But," said the count, interposing, "what has M. Greville to do with it, except as we know that his legation profited by madame's —may I say—interference?"

"I like that," laughed Mrs. Merton, "interference. There is nothing so amiable as the charity of time."

"Ah," said I, laughing, "I, too, had a trifling share in the business. Let us all agree to be frank and to consider as confidential for some years to come what we hear. I am as curious as the countess."

"And no wonder," said the count. "Of course enough got out to make every *chancellerie* in Europe wonder how Mr. Adams was able to report the opinions and even the words of the emperor and his foreign secretary to Lord John."

"Well," said Mrs. Merton, "I am still faintly penitent, but this is a delightful inquisition. Pray go on. I shall be frank."

To begin with, I may presume that you took those papers."

"Stole them," said Mrs. Merton.

"Oh, madame! Why did you not take them at once to Mr. Dayton?"

"I was too scared. I was alarmed when I saw the emperor's handwriting. Was he cross?"

"Oh, I had later a bad quarter of an hour."

"I am sorry. And now you are quite free to tell me next—that I—well, fibbed to you. I did. But lying is not forbidden in the decalogue."

"What about false witness?" cried the countess, amused.

"That hardly covers the ground, but," said Mrs. Merton, "I do not defend myself."

The count laughed. "You did it admirably, and for a half-day I was in doubt. In fact, to confess, I was in such distress that I did not know what to do. The résumé I was to make for the emperor ought to have been

made at the Foréign Office. I was rash
enough to take the papers home."

"But why did you not arrest me at once?"

"Will madame look in the glass for an
answer? You were—well, a lady, your
people loyal, and I was frantic for a day.
I hesitated until I saw you driving toward
the Bois de Boulogne in a storm. What followed you know."

"Yes."

"You concealed the papers, and the police for a while thought you had burned
them. You were clever."

"Not very," said Mrs. Merton. "I tried
to burn all the big double envelops, but the
men hurried me."

"I see," returned the count. "Your ruse,
if it was that, deceived them, delayed things,
and then the papers somehow were removed.
And here my curiosity reaches a climax. It
puzzled me for years, and, as I know, has
puzzled the police."

"But why?" asked I.

"The pistol-shots were, of course, believed to have been a means of decoying away the guard. The old caretaker was found in her room and the room locked. She was greatly alarmed at the cries and the shots, and for a while would not open the door."

Mrs. Merton laughed. "Ah, my good old nurse."

"But the man in charge of the house never left it, or so he said, and the doors, all of them, were locked."

"Indeed!" I exclaimed., "That dear old nurse."

"The police found no trace of what might have been present if a man had entered—I mean muddy footmarks in the house."

"No," I said; "that was pure accident. I took off my shoes when I went in, but with no thought of anything except the noise they might make."

"And," remarked Le Moyne, "of course

any footprints there were outside had been partly worn away by the rain. None of any use were found, and besides for days the police had tramped over every foot of the garden."

"Not to leave you puzzled," said Merton, and really it must have been rather bewildering, I beg that Greville tell you the whole story."

"With pleasure," I said. "Colonel Merton and I were the burglars"; and thereupon I related our adventure.

"No one suspected you," said the count; "but what astonishes me the most is the concealment under a blazing fire of things as easily burned as papers. I see now, but even after the ashes were thrown about by you, the police refused to believe they could have been used to safeguard papers. I should like to tell your story to our old chief of police. He is now retired."

"I see no objection," said I.

"Better not," said Merton. "My wife's share should not, even now, be told."

"You are right," said the countess, "quite right. But how did it occur to you, Madame Merton, to use the ashes as you did?"

"Let me answer," said the colonel. "Any American would know how completely ashes are non-conductors of heat. I knew of their use on one occasion in our Civil War to hide and preserve the safe-conduct of a spy."

"And," said I, "their protective power explains some of the so-called miracles when, as in Japan, men walk over what seems to be a bed of glowing red-hot coals."

"How stupid the losing side appears," said the count, "when one hears all of both sides!"

"But," asked the countess, "how did you get the papers to London? It seems a simple thing, but my husband will tell you that never have there been such extreme measures taken as in this case. The emperor was furious, and yet to the end every one was in the dark."

"You must have played your game well," said Le Moyne.

"Luck is a very good player," I said, "and we had our share."

"Ah, there was more then luck when no amount of cross-questioning could get a word out of Madame Merton."

"My husband insists that I have never been able to make up for that long silence."

We laughed as the count said: "One can jest over it now, but at the time the only amusement I got out of the whole affair was when your dummy envelop came back from London with a savage criticism of the police by our not overpleased embassy in England. I did want to laugh, but M. de Lhuys did not."

"And the original papers?" insisted the countess. "Paris was almost in a state of siege."

"Yes," said her husband, "tell us."

"Well," said I, laughing, "you escorted them to Belgium when we had that affair with Porthos."

"*I!*" exclaimed the count.

"Yes; Colonel Merton insisted on fighting in Belgium merely to enable us to get the papers out of France."

"Indeed! One man did suspect you, but it was too late."

"But Porthos?" cried the countess. "Delightful! Is that the baron?"

"Yes," laughed the count. "My cousin is to this day known as Porthos. But who took the papers? Not you!"

"No, D'Artagnan—I mean, Merton took them as far as Belgium, and then Lieutenant West and I carried them to London. D'Artagnan's share was a bad rapier-wound."

"D'Artagnan?" cried the countess. "That makes it complete."

Merton merely smiled, and the blue eyes narrowed a little as the countess said:

"And so you are D'Artagnan. How delightful! The man of three duels. And pray, who was my husband?"

"That high-minded gentleman, Athos," said Merton, lifting his glass and bowing to the count.

"Gracious!" cried the countess. "What delightfully ingenious people! I shall always call him Athos."

"It was well, colonel," said the count, "that no one suspected you. The absence of secrecy in the duel put the police at fault. Had you been supposed to be carrying those papers, you would never have reached the field."

"Perhaps. One never can tell," said D'Artagnan, simply.

"Ah, well," said our host, rising, "I have long since forgiven you, Madame Merton,

[165]

and no one is now more glad than I that you helped to prevent the recognition of the Confederacy."

"You must permit me to thank you all," said the countess; "my curiosity may now sleep in peace. You were vastly clever folk to have defeated our sharp police."

"Come," said the count, "you Americans will want a cigar. *On peut être fin, mais pas plus fin que tout le monde.*'

www.ingramcontent.com/pod-product-compliance
Lightning Source LLC
LaVergne TN
LVHW091257080426
835510LV00007B/297